Nita's Nibbles: TASTE your BASE!

Written by Vernita Whitaker Naylor

Nita's Nibbles: TASTE your BASE!

Written by Vernita Whitaker Naylor

B.E.S.T Publishing

B.E.S.T
Publishing

Nita's Nibbles: Taste Your Base. Copyright © 2025 by Vernita Whitaker Naylor

All rights reserved and printed in the United States of America. No part of this book, whole or part, may be reproduced via AI, stored in a retrieval system, or transmitted in any form or by any means: electronic, mechanical, photocopying, recording, or otherwise, without written permission from the authors or the publisher except in the case of brief quotations embodied in critical articles and reviews.

Cover Illustration Concept and Design: Nikita Nikol Naylor
Book Illustrations: Nikita Nikol Naylor
Imaging/Photography: Canva Photo Stock Library & Chinaka Hoshi Co.

Library of Congress Cataloging-in-Publication Data

ISBN paperback: 978-0-9915869-4-3
ISBN e-book: 978-0-9915869-5-0

LET'S CONNECT A LITTLE MORE:
Visit our YouTube Channel, Nita's Nibbles @BESTPublishing and other social media platforms, where we offer gardening tips, composting, the best ways to clean your herbs, and much more for your gardening and sustainability lifestyle. For information, updates, or to purchase other B.E.S.T. Publishing products, contact us at jegroup11@gmail.com.

Other books published by

B.E.S.T Publishing

Speaking In Colors

Get the Cheese, Avoid the Traps:
An Interactive Guide to Government Contracting

I am Thankful To All Of You Who Want To Make A Difference Not Only For Your Families But Also To Positively Influence How We Impact The World By Creating A Sustainable Environment.

Eat Healthy.

Be Your Best Selves.

You Are The Change You Were Seeking.

Content

WHAT'S THE STORY BEHIND NITA'S NIBBLES:
    TASTE YOUR BASE?   14

THE INFLUENCE OF MY PARENTS IN MAKING
    THIS COOKBOOK   19

FOOD HAS A MEANING   21
    MY RELATIONSHIP WITH FOOD   22
    HOW FOOD INFLUENCED MY LIFE   24
    IT BEGINS WITH YOUR FOOD   26

FOOD IMPACT ON THE BODY   28
    IS IT JUST ME?   29
    FOOD HAD CHANGED AND I NEEDED TO
        CHANGE WITH IT   30
    GOING BACK 2 BASICS   31
    IS YOUR BODY INFLAMED?   34

Content

WHAT'S GOING ON IN THE KITCHEN?   36
    WHAT DOES **TASTE YOUR BASE** MEAN FOR COOKING?   37
    SUSTAINABILITY & GARDENING   39
    IMPORTANCE OF USING HERBS, SPICES & SEA MOSS FOR TEXTURE   45
    PROPERLY CLEAN YOUR FOOD BEFORE YOU COOK   49

PREPARATION & COOK TIME   51
HELPFUL HINTS   54
    KITCHEN SINK   55
    NOTE   57
    WHAT FLAVORS SUIT YOU?   58

LET'S LOOK INSIDE   60
    BEVERAGES   61
        Heavenly Golden Milk   62
        Healthy Immunity Tonic   63
        Hot Toddy Tonic (For Kids)   65
        Hibiscus Tonic   66
        Mango Lassi   68

Content

SWEETS 69

    Bread Pudding 70

    Homemade Apple Pie 73

    Nita's Buttermilk Lemony Loaf 76

    Oatmeal Spice Cookies 78

    Pineapple Upside Down Cake 81

    Spice Granola Mix 83

BRINE, RUBS & SAUCES 86

    How to Use Brine, Rubs & Sauces 87

    Brine 89

    Japanese Ginger Sauce 90

    Meat Rub 91

    Nita's Nibbles Rub 92

    Nita's Nibbles Spicy! Rub 93

STARTERS 94

    Artichoke & Spinach Dip & Spread 95

    Baked Potato Soup 97

    Broccoli Bake 101

    Butternut Squash 104

    Corn Chowder Soup 109

Content

STARTERS (CONTINUED)
Family's Favorite Cornbread **112**

Groovy Gauc **114**

Jerky Jerk Chicken **117**

Nibble's Mac N Cheese **119**

No Chicken Noodle Soup **121**

Pico Savy Salsa **124**

Turkey Kale Potato Soup **125**

MAIN DISHES **130**
Jamaican & Nigerian Oxtail Stew **131**

Japchae **136**

Lamb in Yogurt Sauce **139**

Chicken Tikka Masala **143**

Vegetable Kadai **146**

Vegetable Thai Yellow Curry **149**

ACKNOWLEDGEMENTS **154**

WHO IS NITA'S NIBBLES? **155**

INDEX **156**

WHAT'S THE STORY BEHIND NITA'S NIBBLES: TASTE YOUR BASE?

The title of this book, Nita's Nibbles: Taste Your Base, holds a special significance. 'Nita is a childhood nickname given to me by my family, friends, and ancestors. It symbolizes a deep connection, warmth, and love.

My ancestors have always watched over and prayed for me, guiding me on my journey, which led me to create this book. People often ask me about my journey as a minimalist and the benefits of a sustainable lifestyle. As I share with many, this cookbook offers a collective glimpse into my world, inviting all to partake.

As Nita, I have intentionally focused most of my life on what goes into my body, how I live, and my impact on Mother Earth. I want to make a difference in the food on my table, which influences how my body functions and operates. Emphasizing sustainable living, healthy eating, and a wellness lifestyle is a crucial starting point.

Each of us has a unique story about our lives and how we live. Reflecting on the impact of our choices can be a powerful tool for personal growth and connection. What story does your life tell?

Sharing our personal stories can inspire others and foster a sense of community, both the good and the bad. It's a reminder that everything we do, who we are, and how we connect with others and Mother Earth are intricately intertwined, which should make us more aware of and responsible for our actions. Everything we do affects how our lives evolve in the future.

This book celebrates the joy of cooking, eating, and sustainability. As part of sustainable living, I take an old saying from my dad, which he always said as I was growing up: 'Nothing in life is to be wasted." So, as I live, eat, and breathe, I focus on keeping these words of wisdom in my heart, mind, and soul.

I'm thrilled to share these quick, easy, and fun dishes with you, and I hope you'll find them as tasty and enjoyable as I do. My dad's wisdom led me to incorporate my 'Kitchen Sink' concept into my cooking. Throughout the book, I will provide 'Kitchen Sink' suggestions.

The concept uses a 'Kitchen Sink' style of cooking, which means making the most of what you already have in your kitchen as a substitute, if needed, for the recipes before purchasing more food to suit the recipe. As you adopt this approach, you will notice reduced food waste and become more creative with your meals. The Kitchen Sink ideas not only help minimize food waste but also emphasize the importance of recycling, repurposing containers, and composting unused food.

It's important to reflect on your steps to reduce food waste and minimize what goes into landfills. Using food scraps, you can reduce waste, create a great compost, and possibly start a small pot garden full of herbs and spices. This is just food for thought.

Nibbling' is a great way to give your organs time to digest your food rather than quickly devouring it or being gluttonous. Intermittent fasting, which means not eating past 3-5 p.m., allows your body to eliminate appropriately. Even when you drink any beverage, sip it so your body can absorb it properly, especially water, which should be consumed at room temperature.

In creating these recipes, you will experience and embrace food through preparation, spices and herbs, culture, history, and returning to basics. Each dish reflects my experiences and tastes, and I hope it will allow you to thoroughly taste the flavors and textures as you nibble and slowly consume them while making them your own.

From the bottom of my heart, thank you for your unwavering commitment to making a positive difference for your family and the world. Your efforts, no matter how small, are invaluable and greatly appreciated. It's because of people like you that we can create a healthier, more sustainable future. Your dedication does not go unnoticed, and I am truly grateful for your support.

"Better health. Better wealth. Better you."
— *Kevin Houston*

THE INFLUENCE OF MY PARENTS IN MAKING THIS COOKBOOK

My parents migrated from the South, Mississippi, and Arkansas to the Bay Area during the Great Migration Era. Many black American families migrated from the South looking for better opportunities. These family travels took them to the West Coast, New York, Chicago, Pennsylvania, and Michigan. Instead of migrating from the South, some families remained in the Southern areas.

My parents brought Southern comfort to Oakland, California (Bay Area), from ideas and lifestyles to foods. Some of these comforts included foods like cornbread, greens, Mac and Cheese, biscuits, black-eyed peas, and different types of veggies, including okra (which I grew to love), beef and pork ribs, chicken, rabbit and squirrel (both of which I refused to eat) and every part of the hog: pig's feet and ears, chitterlings and hog head cheese even pork skins and rinds in the bag with hot sauce. ;-) Looking back, I am happy I remained healthy despite this diet.

One thing that comes to mind is that in those days, the food quality was better and not as tampered with and altered as it is today. Like my dad would always say, "Farm to Table." My mom was an excellent cook, but to be perfectly honest, I had no interest in learning how to cook. Why?

When I was younger, my mom taught my sisters and me how to cook different tasty dishes. When it was my turn, I would intentionally sabotage the meal so I would not be asked to cook again. At the time, watching her cook seemed like an obligation instead of a gift of pleasure.

We never perform to our best abilities when we feel obligated to do anything. Like in high school, one of the assigned classes for females was Home Economics (Home Ec). Home Ec taught gender-specific roles to help us become more well-rounded women when married.

This class taught us a lot, from sewing, housekeeping, budgeting, savings, and healthcare, including preventive care and nutrition to cooking. While I did well in this class, it felt like an obligation. Little did I know that learning these tasks, including cooking at home with my mom and in class, would become a significant part of my life.

FOOD HAS A MEANING

MY RELATIONSHIP WITH FOOD

It appeared that cooking was at the forefront everywhere I turned, from home to school, yet it always felt like an obligation. Yes, learning how to cook from my mom and embracing what was taught in Home Ec was essential for my survival and necessary to obtain a passing grade, but at the time, I didn't see it that way.

Fast-forward: I married and became a mother at 19. Ironically, my husband loved to cook; go figure! I saw in him the pleasure of creating, cooking, and serving. Watching him cook gave me the vibes of someone with a good relationship with food.

As he cooked, you saw the love, fun, and enjoyment without the essence of feeling obligated. He would have great pleasure in watching me taste these delectable dishes, which, ironically, weren't the dishes but the flavors and spices that I connected with and reminded me of home. His take on cooking was fantastic, and it increased my desire and taste for food, turning me into a true foodie.

As I became more acquainted with the taste of these foods, I was excited to learn more about them. During my marriage, I had the opportunity to taste all types of tasty dishes from various cultures, from America and Asia to Africa. His dishes and those of my upbringing inspired me to provide you with some of my favorite recipes.

I discovered that many of the same herbs and spices were used by different cultures for various dishes, yet they still had the same health and healing properties. When we divorced, I was back to the task of cooking and had to figure things out quickly. What is a girl to do with no cooking skills?

There were few options available, so I had to choose between learning how to cook and saving money or being broke eating out every day. I must admit that initially, I would regularly patronize fast food spots and high-end restaurants in the Bay Area, which became an expensive habit. Still, it was sometimes worth it because the Bay Area had excellent food from various cultures.

But as eating out cost me money, I wondered why I could not return to the basics of what my mom and Home Ec had been trying to teach me. Funny, after all this eating out, my daughter developed a silver-spoon food palette. The nerve of her!

My relationship with food has caused me to occasionally indulge in a small portion of sweets before my meal. It's a delightful way to start a meal. Why not have a little fun first?! So, for my guilty pleasure, you will see that I start my cookbook unconventionally, with sweets and beverages before the main meals.

What is your relationship with food and the stories behind them? Tell us your guilty pleasure.

HOW FOOD INFLUENCED MY LIFE

As I reflected on returning back to basics, I began reminiscing about living in the Bay Area. People in the Bay Area had a beautiful vibe, were friendly and relaxed. We had terrific athletes, musicians, visual artists and other types of creatives.

Our creative artists, musically or through visual expression, exuded a flow and essence that told many stories about life in the Bay; this was the same with our food. Growing up in the Bay Area, every meal was an adventure. The culinary scene was a vibrant tapestry of flavors and cultures, each dish a testament to the diverse backgrounds of those who brought their recipes with them.

Within a 15–25-minute radius, you could easily find restaurants serving delicious foods from Caribbean, Jamaican, Asian, Mexican, Ethiopian, African, and Soul Food to Italian, each dish bursting with the unique notes of its herbs and spices. It was a joy to discover new flavors and dishes, each a delightful surprise. There were also many delectable desserts, ice cream, chocolate, and treats within the same area.

Everything smelled delicious and looked and tasted like a symphony of flavors and textures. The eating experience was not just about the food but the surrounding sights, smells, and sounds. Just like these restaurants or food trucks were the places where you would experience beautiful flavors, spices, and textures, this was the same when you would visit someone's home for dinner, attend a backyard event, meet at the park, beach, lake, marina, or any spot where the common goal is for people to come together to connect, laugh, catch up, and eat good food.

Good food has always been a powerful memory trigger for me. A few other places where I had the pleasure of having good food experiences were New York, Arizona, New Orleans, and various Countries I've visited. So, I know good food when I taste, see, and smell it.

Going back to basics was a good thing for me because I had many beautiful food experiences. I cherish and reflect on these experiences and the memories they created. How has food influenced your life? Let's celebrate the diversity and richness of our food culture together as I invite you to join me in this reflection journey.

IT BEGINS WITH YOUR FOOD

The taste of your food begins with its quality. To ensure you have high-grade, flavorful, and tasty dishes, you must focus on where, when, and how you purchase your food. You may or may not have noticed that if you go to your corner or convenience store, for example, and pick up some fruits or vegetables and smell them, it lacks the essence of what you're looking for because the zest is lacking.

Once you cook the food, you will see that the quality and taste could have been better. While a corner or convenience store is readily available to purchase things like fruits, vegetables, herbs, spices, baked goods, eggs, dairy, or meat, focus on doing some planning on your part and visit a:

- Cooperative or Farmer's Market;
- Participate in a Community Supported Agriculture (CSA) Program;
- Bakery;
- Small businesses that may offer specialty items;
- Build a relationship with a farmer who may also provide produce, eggs, and a
- Butcher.

Some places have surpluses that can benefit your family's needs and must be sold before they spoil or become outdated. Frequenting these places can also develop relationships, which can be a win-win for everyone involved. Wherever you decide to get your food, research the facts to help determine the right choices for you and your family.

This informed decision-making process puts the power in your hands when providing for your family. Choose wisely and feel empowered by your responsible choices. Another rewarding option is to grow your food or build a farm.

Whether it's a small garden or a community project, the satisfaction of cultivating and harvesting your produce and food is unparalleled. The taste and texture of the food you grow yourself is a testament to your hard work and dedication. Trust me, it will be rewarding!

As we delve further into the book, you will learn that having quality foods impacts how your food smells, looks, tastes, and affects your body. One crucial thing to remember is that you MUST Taste Your Base as you create the beautiful dishes in this book. It's all about the sensory experience while cooking with quality ingredients.

This connection to your food is what makes cooking a truly rewarding experience. What are some local restaurants, bakeries, cafés, farmer's markets, or butchers that you would like to Shout Out? Share with us, and don't forget to provide their website or contact information so we can patronize them. By sharing your experiences, you're promoting these businesses and fostering a sense of community among us all.

FOOD IMPACT ON THE BODY

IS IT JUST ME?

Let's take a trip down memory lane, shall we? Remember when food seemed to have a richer, more satisfying flavor? And who could forget the allure of a cold, refreshing Coca-Cola? It wasn't just a drink; it was an experience.

As I became a young adult, somebody told me that Coca-Cola back then contained cocaine. Go figure! I am not sure how true this is, but it was so refreshing compared to the taste now, which is full of sugar, and the taste could be better.

It's not just you. Have you ever noticed that the sight and smell of food can significantly influence your perception of its taste? When a dish looks and smells appetizing, it's like a prelude to a symphony of flavors that your taste buds already anticipate.

Due to the lack of quality and flavors, I no longer consume soft drinks or eat many foods I once did. This disappointment led me to focus on cooking dishes I enjoy, where I control the quality and flavors. What about you?

What is different about how you look at what you eat or drink today versus in the past? What changes have you noticed in your relationship with food and beverages? We'd love to hear your story, so please share it with us on our social media platforms.

FOOD HAD CHANGED AND I NEEDED TO CHANGE WITH IT

In the late 1990s and early 2000s, the quality and taste of foods gradually changed and became compromised, from the delightful dishes in restaurants and fast-food chains to the offerings in grocery stores. The lack of flavors and textures that were once a part of my childhood slowly faded away, leaving a sense of nostalgia for those delicious quality dishes I had taken for granted. As they say, you never realize how much you miss something until it's gone. So true!

My colonic therapist constantly reminded me that one thing that remains constant is the struggle to maintain a healthy quality of life. I began to consider where I brought my food. I was also reminded of my dad and how he always had something growing in the backyard, from limes, oranges, apples, plums, and walnuts to how he composted.

Fast-forward to now: As a foodie slowly approaching my late 40s and early 50s, I focused on what it would take to maintain good health while taking the steps necessary to grow old gracefully. Keeping with me the words of wisdom from my colonic therapist and my dad and his connection with the Earth. I realized that life provided me with the answers; I always sought but was waiting for me to embrace it.

Never in my wildest dreams would I see myself living and fully committing to this lifestyle of eating, thinking, and connecting with Mother Nature and food. While I may sometimes go off course, and my practices are not always perfect, I am committed to a minimalistic lifestyle. I have a long way to go, but I am dedicated to executing sustainable practices and finding ways to connect, embrace, and give back to the Earth. To stay on the path, I must intentionally execute these goals daily, a commitment that I hope inspires others.

GOING BACK 2 BASICS

Every part of me and my lifestyle begins with my upbringing, but let me explain how it all ties together. Like most families who migrated from the South, my parents focused on the necessities. These ideas were the gems I later incorporated into my life and were responsible for raising my daughter.

Embracing a holistic lifestyle was a journey of empowerment for me. It meant simplifying and returning to the fundamental health and wellness principles. It's about embracing natural, unprocessed foods, sustainable living practices, and mindful consumption.

This journey has enriched my life and inspired me to share my experiences with you, hoping to ignite a similar sense of empowerment in your journey. My mother, a pivotal figure in my holistic journey, raised me on foods from the health food store. The book Back to Eden by Jethro Kloss, which I still use today, was my food Bible.

As I got older, I delved into other books like Healing Secrets of the Native Americans: Herbs, Remedies, and Practices that Restore the Body, Refresh the Mind, and Rebuild the Spirit by Porter Shimer and Eat Right For Your Blood Type by Dr. Peter J. D'Adamo. I was allergic to too many things to count, from various foods to medication; it felt like I lived in a bubble. I am sure that some of you who have or are still experiencing eczema, psoriasis, or other auto-immune diseases or nervous system disorders can relate.

My mother did an excellent job using various processes and methods to ensure I lived a healthy life with minimal flare-ups. She also minimized my allergic triggers, allowing my body to develop a healthier immune system. I still have some allergic triggers, but over time, the systems that she created allowed me to benefit from them today.

While I can now eat most of the foods that I was once allergic to because my immune system is robust, I still avoid as many of these allergens or triggers as possible. About 20-25 years ago, I began drinking raw, unpasteurized milk and returned to drinking goat's milk. I started incorporating other goat products like goat's butter and occasionally use goat body butter for the skin.

This shift, part of my holistic lifestyle, has brought many benefits. My best-laid plan of Going Back To Basics is working out for my good, and I hope it can inspire you to consider similar changes. I didn't know that living a holistic, minimalistic, sustainable lifestyle was a movement at the time, but it impacted my relationships in every way, including my relationship with money and how I spent it.

Immediately, I began to visit the butcher and the farmer's market more, especially within the Berkeley area. Over time, I started to see patterns when talking to others about how they cooked and lived, especially among many immigrants who lived in the Bay Area. Then, as I began to move to other States, another thing that I took for granted was sustainability.

The Bay Area was significant in terms of sustainable living, including recycling, which is minor in other states. I appreciated and actively participated in these practices, from composting to reducing waste. While imperfect and with a long way to go, my lifestyle allows me to execute sustainable practices and find ways to connect, embrace, and give back to the Earth.

So, no matter where I lived, I embraced recycling and sustainable living more while transitioning into a fluid, minimalistic lifestyle. Everything began to fall into place, from eating and my health to my lifestyle. My love for food led me to cultivate the Kitchen Sink idea and my dad's words of wisdom 'Nothing is To Be Wasted.'

This journey enriched my palate and deepened my appreciation. I hope to share this sense of enrichment with you through my experiences and recipes, encouraging you to embrace the diversity that enriches the culinary experience. My journey with food and recipes provided an outlet for connecting to my past and the future.

Cooking no longer felt like an obligation or a chore. This channel of mastering dishes can inspire you to embark on your culinary adventures, feeling the same sense of accomplishment and connection that I do. As they say, all things work as they should, and some come back full circle.

Through these pages, I hope you cultivate a life of love, optimal health, healing, and positive energy, whether you're beginning or have been on your holistic journey for some time. Reflect on some of your Back to Basic moments that you are beginning to incorporate into your life.

Thank you for joining me on this pathway. Each of our experiences is valuable and can inspire others. As we believe in the power of shared experiences in our holistic journey, let's continue to give the support necessary to make a difference in the world.

IS YOUR BODY INFLAMED?

While we often focus on our external appearance, caring for our internal health is equally important. Consuming the wrong foods, such as processed sugars, trans fats, and excessive red meat, can neglect our internal well-being and result in various health conditions, from dental issues, including bad breath, digestive problems, and sore throats to migraines. Excessive inflammation, which many are unaware of as the root cause, is also responsible for frequent bouts of mucus, colds, flu, and other autoimmune diseases.

The same applies to those impacted by COVID-19, which ended not long ago and is allegedly resurfacing. If your body was heavily inflamed, you were most likely struck hard with this illness. COVID-19 and inflammation make your body struggle to breathe fluidly and unable to recover quickly, similar to having asthma. The inflammatory response triggered by COVID-19 can lead to severe respiratory issues and other complications, making it crucial to manage inflammation for better health.

Today, some people are still living with and working through COVID-related issues and complications, and I am sure that inflammation is playing a massive part in this. Whenever I am highly inflamed due to allergens or overindulging with specific types of foods, I tend to have achy joints, especially knees, and an upset stomach, including bloating, skin rashes, and even headaches. None of these conditions are a normal part of my life, so when this occurs, it is a clear sign that I am inflamed and must take action.

When my body becomes inflamed, I take action to alleviate it by either making a fruit smoothie with water or coconut water as my base, drinking hot tea, going on a fast, or eating soup, I do whatever my body needs to decrease the excess mucus or inflammation. Living with any illness, especially those living with COVID-related, can be challenging, but knowing that I can take steps to manage my inflammation gives me hope and keeps me motivated. Trying to get back to normal for many is also a challenge.

The pandemic caused many people to be sheltered, fearful, and isolated, and many of us began to create a paradigm shift in how we lived our lives moving forward. I started concentrating more on staying healthy, so I returned to my childhood methods. The books I mentioned that my mom used, which I eventually began to use more frequently as an adult for guidance, especially Back to Eden, have always been helpful.

These personal experiences have shaped the health strategies I use today, and I believe they can benefit others as well. The book Eat Right For Your Blood Type has also been essential because it has helped me use blood type principles to reduce inflammation. As I concentrate on my blood type, I continue to learn about the beneficial and detrimental things that can impact my body.

I've also learned that genetics, culture, environment, and other factors also affect and influence how the body processes everything we encounter. Removing as much inflammation or triggers as possible from our bodies and surroundings is essential to our overall health. Through continual practice, these methods and principles minimize the amount of inflammation entering the body and offer several benefits, from not being and living on medication to experiencing a better quality of life.

Taking care of your body and maintaining a healthy lifestyle is a great start. Think about what you are doing to avoid being so inflamed. Your experiences and strategies are valuable.

WHAT'S GOING ON IN THE KITCHEN?

WHAT DOES <u>TASTE YOUR BASE</u> MEAN FOR COOKING?

Never underestimate the power of tasting your base. It's not just a step in cooking; it's a crucial element that can make or break your dish. Your base is the heart and soul of your food; by tasting it, you're setting the stage for the entire culinary experience.

This simple act of tasting and adjusting will give you confidence and control over your cooking, ensuring your dish turns out just how you want it. Visualize the taste you want to achieve, and make sure the flavors, spices, smells, and textures are all in harmony. Before adding other ingredients, give your base a chance to settle.

You will notice that executing this step will allow the flavors to meld and ensure that no single taste overpowers the dish from being too spicy, salty, sweet, or bland. If you're happy with the base, that's great. If not, gradually add more 'base' ingredients until you achieve the perfect taste.

Once your base is set and ready to begin cooking, you'll notice a section labeled 'Ready To Mix.' This is not just a set of Cooking Directions or Cooking Instructions; it's a space to have fun, get excited, and fully engage in the process. So, get ready to mix and let the culinary adventure begin.

Enjoy the journey of creating something delicious from scratch. Always remember to TASTE YOUR BASE!

SUSTAINABILITY & GARDENING

To stay on the path to minimizing inflammation within my body while making a difference in my connection with Mother Earth, I returned to my Back to Basic principles. As a foodie, I continued to embark on an adventure in longing for delicious foods that possessed quality, embraced good health, were nutritious, and embodied flavor. To help me along this journey, I decided to grow a garden.

My garden is not just a patch of green but a symbol of control and empowerment. It allows me to dictate what goes into my body, using organic methods and systems that positively impact the Earth. This sense of control, coupled with the incorporation of sustainability, makes sustainable living essential for my lifestyle.

Sustainable living has made me mindful of how I impact Mother Earth, which in turn has empowered me to make a difference. What each of us does today influences the Earth and future generations. We can take action by using our daily resources, making a difference, and taking it one step at a time.

Using our resources efficiently can make our lives easier and is the best thing to do. One of those things is looking at what goes into your garbage can. For example, instead of weekly, our trash is picked up only twice a month because we try to recycle and reuse everything:

- Aluminum inc cans and foil;
- All types of plastic inc bottles;
- Paper inc boxes used for garden or composting;
- Glass inc bottles;
- Electronics on occasion; and
- Most of our food scraps, except animal meat products

We go to the recycling facility about three to four times a month. We separate our aluminum, plastic, paper, glass, and electronics by category using several oversized bags for easy disposal, except for the boxes and electronics, which are too large for a bag. Just imagine the impact that your family doing the same thing would have on the landfill.

After each recycling run, we feel a wave of accomplishment and fulfillment. Everything we recycle makes our garage and house feel lighter, not just physically but also in spirit. Depending on the type of glass or plastic container we wish to discard, we may consider repurposing it for other uses, such as marinating or storing our dry rubs, harvested herbs, spices, and, at times, rainwater.

We feel great satisfaction as we continue on this sustainable journey. As a child, I began to see the value of repurposing items, and I recall watching my dad do the same thing. He used this method not only to store leftovers in the refrigerator but also for his tools.

Even though he had many types of toolboxes, he would store his wrenches, screws and nuts, hammers, and other items in various kinds of containers, including old paint buckets. So, I used some of the same principles: we repurpose our unused boxes for our garden instead of recycling them. We prune the weeds and wildflowers around the garden beds, then place cardboard down to suppress anything that tries to grow in the soil around the beds and add garden rocks.

For the fallen leaves, limbs, and branches scattered in the yard, we place them in a trash can to decompose and use them during the gardening season or burn them in our outdoor firepit on those cold days, along with fallen pine cones that we gather. If you take the time to recycle, you will discover that within three, six, nine, and twelve months, you and your family have made a tremendous dent in reducing greenhouse gases.

Recycling materials like paper, plastic, glass, and metal reduces the need for new raw materials, conserves energy, and decreases greenhouse gas emissions.

These gases are released into the air, dramatically impacting our quality of life. Recycling will cause you to notice how much plastic is being manufactured for our daily use. Due to its inability to decompose quickly, plastic significantly impacts the landfill and Mother Earth.

In the Bay Area, we had a recycling program, which my family took advantage of. This helped give me another perspective on sustainability. If your city or state doesn't have a recycling program, a recycling facility may be nearby.

Do your part to help change the climate. You will notice the difference that one person or family can make. Now, let's focus more on the importance of gardening as it pertains to sustainability.

My gardening journey recalls me back to watching my dad take food scraps and create a compost for his garden. I only knew what he was doing once I got older. He would throw scraps in the corner out in the open, which looked nasty, especially when they broke down.

This way of life, he said, reminded him of home in Mississippi, where 'Nothing Is To Be Wasted.' I never saw him turn the pile, but I noticed that his apples, oranges, plums, and lemons were always flavorful and sweet. Looking back, I took these simple life lessons for granted but understood that it was all part of the process.

Gardening became one of the best decisions I've ever made, beginning with composting and preparing the seeds or plants to be used. Composting is recycling materials you usually would have around your house to formulate rich soil for your garden. Think of compost as vitamins and minerals needed for the body to function effectively.

We created a compost bed about the size of our garden beds. To have rich compost soil, continually think of this formula:

A balance of brown and green material such as grass clippings, food scraps (except for dairy and meats), occasionally coffee grounds, tea bags, cardboard, paper, toilet rolls, leaves, and egg shells plus water, heat, and turning everything at least once a week (frequency depends upon the decomposition) = earthworms and beautiful, earthy soil that feels and smells wonderful. We add fallen tree limbs and branches to the bottom of the compost so that everything can breathe and generate the appropriate heat. sometimes, we add a cover over the entire bed to create more heat when needed.

In our kitchen, we have repurposed holding containers with lids, where we put our food scraps, including fruit and egg shells, for later composting. Since adopting my dad's mantra, 'Nothing Is To Be Wasted,' I have learned how to balance the green and brown materials, know when to add water, how often to turn the compost, and so much more. This journey of discovery, learning from research, and joining social media gardening groups has been a source of remarkable personal growth.

Gardening has allowed me to grow plants, brought me back to basics and my roots, cultivated a deeper relationship with nature, and connected me with my ancestors, my dad, and my childhood in many ways. Just thinking about how my journey evolved, bridging sustainability and gardening, makes me smile! It has guided and led me to cultivate, develop, and care for nature's beauty.

I grow all types of things in my garden, from herbs to various vegetables. This sense of connection with nature is one of the most rewarding aspects of my gardening journey. In creating my garden, I consider everything for sustainability, from the soil, seeds, plantings, harvest, and composting to collecting rainwater.

Living a sustainable lifestyle, from recycling to gardening, can seem problematic initially because it's a lot of work and time-consuming, but it's worth it. However, if you make it a beautiful part of your life instead of looking at it as work, the results will be rewarding! Imagine eating the foods YOU have cultivated organically while being kind to Mother Earth.

Your body will thank you for it. Enjoy the process. Like my dad, 'Nothing Is To Be Wasted!'

"Nothing Is To Be Wasted!"
Vertis Whitaker

IMPORTANCE OF USING
HERBS, SPICES & SEA MOSS FOR TEXTURE

As you journey through this book, you'll discover that I often use the same ingredients to enrich my dishes. What's truly remarkable is that many of these herbs and spices I hold dear are also integral to various cultural cuisines, from Africa, Mexico, and Asia to Brazil. This shared culinary heritage adds a unique depth and richness to our cooking:

- allspice
- basil
- cardamon
- cayenne, chili pepper or paprika
- cinnamon
- cumin
- curry
- garlic
- ginger
- lemon pepper
- nutmeg
- onion
- oregano
- rosemary
- sea moss
- thyme
- turmeric

These herbs and spices aren't just ingredients to me; they're a part of my heritage. They bring to life the flavors and textures cherished by my ancestors and are still celebrated in various cultures today. Fresh herbs and spices offer more benefits and taste better, but you can also use them, dried or ground.

Herbs and spices are not just flavor enhancers but also powerhouses of health benefits. With over twenty-five years of experience using these ingredients, I can vouch for their role in promoting a healthy body, reducing inflammation and even eliminating the need for medication. Another dish staple is unflavored sea moss, a versatile ingredient with numerous health benefits, including its role as a food thickener.

Whether you are a vegan or looking for a substitute, sea moss can be used instead of eggs and/or butter. We make our sea moss, but you can purchase it in its original form or as a gel at your local health food store or farmer's market. Here are some benefits of using herbs and spices, and sea moss: anti-oxidant and anti-inflammation properties, improved digestive health, immune system booster, stimulates weight loss, anti-cancer, joint mobility, lower blood sugar, brain health, relieves muscle pain and stiffness, anti-bacterial, lowers cholesterol, supports thyroid function, reduce arthritis symptoms, minimize anxiety; improves kidney, gut and heart health; improve mood and sleep functions, and so much more.

Spices and herbs are essential for the texture of the dish, so if my garden doesn't have what I need for my dish, one of my favorite go-to places is the ethnic markets (Asian, African, Indian, and the like), which have the beautiful flavors I require.

Depending on the dish, I only use Himalayan, Kosher, or Sea Salt, which requires a pinch to a teaspoon. These salts offer a robust flavor to the dish. The salt you choose is your choice; this is only a suggestion.

When it comes to sugar, brown sugar is my personal preference. This preference was solidified during my visit to Ghana, where brown sugar was the only option. They only had a few sweets and desserts, compared to the States. When I had tea during my visit, brown sugar was readily available; I've been using it for everything that requires sweetening ever since.

When you add herbs, spices, salt, or sugar, especially if they are of excellent quality and highly concentrated, you must Taste Your Base and let the dish settle (sit). Letting the dish settle allows the flavors to crystalize, thus enhancing the dish and preventing it from being overwhelmed. If you don't allow the dish to settle and then Taste Your Base before adding more, your dish may become too salty or sweet.

When I've resorted to using subpar ingredients from the grocery store, my dishes often fell short, necessitating several adjustments to achieve the desired flavors, textures, and taste. Always be mindful of what you include in your dishes. The lesson here is clear: the quality of your produce and ingredients matters.

Consider where you source your food and what goes into your dishes. Investing in high-quality ingredients will elevate your cooking and make your dishes stand out. Your palette and body will thank you for it.

PROPERLY CLEAN YOUR FOOD

PROPERLY CLEAN YOUR FOOD BEFORE YOU COOK

Regardless of where you purchase your foods, cleaning them is a powerful act of self-care, especially for rice, beans, fruits, vegetables, and meat. By taking control of the cleanliness of our food, we can't be sure about the quality control and cleanliness protocol of the companies that manufacture and distribute our food. This empowers us to take control of our health, safety, and well-being.

Rice: Depending on how much rice you are making, add just enough water to cover the top of the rice. For example, add one cup of rice and approximately one and ¼ cups of water in a small bowl. Let the rice sit overnight or for about thirty minutes in the refrigerator.

Stir the rice around a little, and you will notice a white or light film over it. Repeat the process, if necessary, until the white film is gone. Now the rice is ready to cook.

Beans: The bean process is similar to preparing your rice, but allow the beans to sit overnight or for about 45-60 minutes in the refrigerator. As the beans sit, you'll notice that all the water is gone and the beans are swollen. Also, you may see some dirt or grit at the bottom of the bowl. Don't worry, this is normal.

Transfer the beans to another bowl to clean, rinse, and remove all dirt and grit, especially at the bottom. Repeat the cleaning process as needed. Now, the beans are ready to cook.

Remember, the cleaner the beans, the softer they will be. If they are soft, they will cook quickly and easily, giving your dishes a great taste.

Fruits & Vegetables: If you have a lot of produce (separate your fruits and vegetables), place them in a medium to large bowl with 1/4 cup vinegar. Let everything sit for 1-2 minutes, then massage the produce in the water solution. As you massage the produce you will experience the satisfaction of removing dirt, wax, pesticides, and grime, knowing that you are preparing safe and healthy food for your loved ones.

Drain the mixture from the bowl, then add just enough water to cover the produce in the bowl. Let it sit for about 3 minutes, massage, then drain the water. Repeat the process if needed. Prepare the produce as needed. Remember, each produce requires a container for proper cleaning.

Meat: Depending upon how much meat you are preparing and the size of the beef (rack of ribs on the bone vs. chicken wings), in a bowl or pan large enough to hold the meat, add 1-2 tablespoons of vinegar to two cups of water. This solution is ideal for up to 3-5 lbs. If you clean a larger quantity of meat, increase the water by 1/2 cup with 1/2 tablespoon of vinegar.

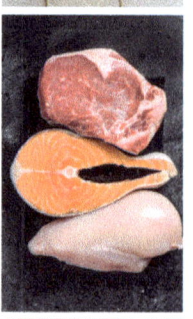

Place the meat in the pan's water solution, begin massaging, and clean it for a few minutes. Drain the mixture from the bowl, add enough water to cover the meat, and massage again without vinegar. Remove the meat from the water in the bowl, pat dry if needed, then prepare.

PREPARATION & COOK TIME

PREPARATION & COOK TIME

PREPARATION:

Cooking can be fun or seem like a chore; the choice is yours. To enjoy the essence of cooking, you must take the steps necessary to minimize your downtime when preparing a dish. If you're like me, you may need to prepare meals quickly.

Sometimes, I'm in the zone, effortlessly whipping up a meal in the kitchen. But when I'm not feeling it, I turn to my trusty prep time method. This method not only streamlines the process but also gives me a sense of control, empowering me to set things up ahead of time and cook with confidence:

- I lay out my herbs, spices, and base ingredients to ensure I have everything I need. This efficient process helps me identify missing items or potential substitutions, boosting my productivity. This is when the Kitchen Sink method comes in handy (See Kitchen Sink method under Helpful Hints section);
- Then, after 10-20 minutes or more, I set out the other ingredients to see if I have everything else required. At that point, I can determine if I need to purchase something or make another substitution using the Kitchen Sink method;
- I begin cleaning the ingredients and chopping up everything, and
- Next, I ensure that all the necessary cookware, including utensils, measuring cups and spoons, pots, pans, and baking dishes, is cleaned and available.

Once these steps have been performed, the recipes take approximately 30 minutes unless something needs to sit for hours or overnight. We're all on this cooking journey together, and sharing tips and tricks can help us all become better and more efficient cooks. So, please share your preparation methods with us. Your unique approach could inspire someone else's cooking adventure.

COOKING:

It's essential to consider your oven type when cooking, as they vary in temperature. My electric stove operates differently than gas, so it's essential to be mindful. The same thing is to consider this principle when using any appliance, from the burner to an air fryer.

Despite the time stated for cooking, always carefully watch your food to avoid undercooking, overcooking or burning. This also applies when using a kitchen gadget like a blender or Nutribullet to mix, pulse, or blend your ingredients.

KITCHEN SINK

Using what you have in your kitchen is essential. There is a lot of food waste that could benefit those who are impoverished, or homeless within the U.S, or other Countries. We either buy too much, desire something else, never use it, let it spoil, or throw it away.

So, a Kitchen Sink is a concept that represents ways to use what you already have in your pantry or refrigerator to accompany many dishes while avoiding and minimizing food waste. Several suggestions will be made to help you choose foods that you may already have readily available before making other food purchases. As you create some of these dishes, you will see food differently and continue to look for ways to be creative.

It is highly recommended that you create 2-3xs more sauce or freeze some of the dishes, including the meat, to be used later. The frozen sauces and dishes will still be delicious once you reheat them. Have fun with this process.

Here are some Kitchen Sink ideas that I created on the fly using what was in my refrigerator:

Occasionally, when I visit a restaurant and have leftovers, I think of ways to continue the experience. Whenever I get Pho, vegetable curry, or other dishes and extra juice is left, I think of how to use it. One day, I got some Vegetable Pho, which usually has a lot of juice left.

As I pondered over the juice, I embarked on a flavor adventure in my refrigerator. I was mindful that any addition could subtly alter the original taste, but I was excited to see how it would enhance the dish. I added mushrooms, onion, carrots, and basil, along with some amino acids and peanut sauce, creating a dish that was a delightful blend of flavors.

I knew that adding cucumber, celery, bell pepper, and other similar vegetables from my refrigerator would give the dish a different taste than I was aiming for. I let everything simmer and settle, then Taste My Base, and it was awesome. I felt a sense of accomplishment in creating another unique dish that perfectly embodied the flavors I was aiming for.

Here's another one. I have a soft spot for pizza. I always keep a thin-crust pizza crust in my pantry.

One day, I experimented and added carrots, lettuce, tomatoes, onion, bell pepper, mushroom, and tomato sauce, but no cheese. It was a revelation to discover the unique taste that emerged, a taste that I had never experienced before. It was an acquired taste that I was glad to have discovered using food around the house.

Another time, I wanted more vegetables in my fried rice, so I added more vegetables along with my fried rice base sauce that I made a few months ago. The sauce was stored in a repurposed glass container in the refrigerator. I sauteed everything in my Wok and let it settle.

Wow, what a treat! As you can see, "Nothing Is To Be Wasted" There are so many ways to get creative and use what you already have to develop excellent dishes that you and your family will enjoy.

Please share your experience with us. Thank you for helping us eliminate food waste and for being a part of the sustainability family.

NOTE

Some recipes include insightful notes. These notes are not just helpful; they are your secret weapon to making informed cooking decisions and streamlining the cooking process. They will guide you in making low-dairy choices, reveal how chili pepper and paprika can elevate your dishes, and demystify the differences between broth and bouillon.

The note section will also provide you with food for thought about the dish, allowing you to make the most of the dish while enhancing your cooking experience. Additionally, there will be some substitution suggestions for you to consider. Carefully read the whole recipe and, specifically, the note section before proceeding with the recipe.

WHAT FLAVORS SUIT YOU?

Are you ready to dive into the world of flavors? Food's taste, smell, appearance, and texture are crucial in your culinary experiences. Whether it's a dish from your favorite restaurant or a creation in your kitchen, the right flavors can elevate the experience.

Unleash your culinary creativity with the versatile nature of certain flavors. Soy Sauce, amino acids, and Tamari, with their ability to enhance a wide range of dishes, will inspire you and empower you to experiment and innovate in your kitchen. Whether you are familiar with one or interested in trying them all, explore!

Delve deeper into the world of flavors and their profound impact on your food. Soy Sauce, with its thin consistency and slight salt taste, amino acids, and Tamari, similar to soy sauce but with unique characteristics, will pique your interest and enhance your culinary knowledge. Let's delve into some practical applications.

Soy Sauce, for instance, can be used in stir-fries, marinades, and dipping sauces. Amino acids, with their mild flavor, are great for seasoning salads, steamed vegetables, and grilled meats. Similar to Soy Sauce it has a stronger flavor.

Tamari is perfect for adding depth to soups, stews, and sauces. Imagine a hearty miso soup with a splash of Tamari or a fresh salad drizzled with amino acids for a burst of umami flavor. Tamari is thicker and has a much stronger flavor than amino acids, with a bit of sweetness.

At first, I preferred Soy Sauce due to the flavors I've come to enjoy, whether in a restaurant or when prepping my food. About a few years ago, I noticed that my tastebuds had been calling for the flavors of amino acids, so this is now my go-to flavor.

I remember the first time I experimented with Tamari in a stew and how it transformed the dish with its rich, umami flavor. As stated in the Kitchen Sink and Notes sections of the recipes, you can, in most cases, use what you have, but be prepared to get creative in making the flavors, texture, and tastes your own. Again, you will notice that in this cookbook, some recipes call for some of the same types of foods, herbs and spices.

Let's Look Inside

BEVERAGES

Heavenly Golden Milk

> When I wish to enhance my meals, especially those with a bit of heat and beautiful spices, I may add this treat afterward with coconut milk and brown sugar. Occasionally, I may drink this beverage alone, especially on cold and rainy days or if I am experiencing an upset stomach.

INGREDIENTS
BASE:

- 3 tbsp turmeric (ground)
- 1 tsp ginger (ground)
- 1 tsp cinnamon (ground)
- 1 tsp allspice (ground)
- 1 tsp nutmeg (ground)
- 1/8 tsp anise (ground)
- Pinch or 1/8 tsp black pepper (ground)
- 1 tsp cardamon (ground) – optional
- ½ tsp vanilla extract – optional

READY TO MIX:

Mix all of the spices in a small bowl and blend thoroughly. Taste Your Base and add anything you desire if needed. Place the ingredients in a small, airtight, repurposed glass container and put it in the pantry.

When you are ready to drink, heat one cup of dairy or non-dairy milk and add your favorite sweetener. Taste Your Base to ensure that it has the desired flavor. Add additional ingredients if needed.

Makes about three cups using approximately one teaspoon. Suitable for about 60 days.

Healthy Immunity Tonic

Many people take medication for anything and everything, but they don't realize that focusing on preventive care is the first step to living a healthy life. As the weather changes, so should your daily regimens, from liquid intake and what you eat to how you care for your skin. My tonic helps boost your immune system by reducing inflammation, especially during the spring and winter seasons when our respiratory system is challenged more due to pollen, air pollution, and other environmental issues.

INGREDIENTS
BASE:

- 4.5 cups lime juice or 1 cup freshly squeezed lime
- 8-9 cups cold or warm water (juice) or 4 cups cold or warm water (squeezed)
- 2 cups honey or 1.5 cups agave (according to taste)
- 7 slivers of raw garlic
- 1 tbsp raw ginger (sliced)
- 1 tbsp ginger (ground)
- 2 tsp red pepper/cayenne pepper
- 1/2 tsp turmeric (ground)
- 1-2 tsp sea moss - optional

NOTE:

If you add the two teaspoons of pepper as suggested, you will have "heat" which is suitable forth e respiratory and immune systems. However, if you do not want a "lot" of heat, add only one teaspoon of the red/cayenne pepper.

HEALTHY IMMUNITY TONIC (CONTINUED)

Due to its properties and potency, only one cup is needed once a week. However, if you must take more due to excessive inflammation, take no more than ½ cup three (3) times a week, preferably every other day, to allow your system to make the necessary adjustments.

READY TO MIX:

Mix the Base Ingredients in a large pitcher in the order listed and stir to ensure that flavors blend nicely. Let the ingredients sit for about 30 minutes. Taste Your Base. Strengthening your base ingredients is essential here, but remember that the tonic should have a bitter-sweet consistency. If you need more flavor, gradually add more.

Hot Toddy Tonic (FOR KIDS)

This recipe is similar to the Healthy Immunity Tonic but ideal for children under 12. It is designed to help build their immune system while reducing inflammation. Children are highly influenced by the weather and the surrounding elements, from pollen to air pollution.

INGREDIENTS
BASE:

- 2 cups lime juice or 1/2 cup freshly squeezed lime
- 4 cups cold or warm water (juice) or 2 cups cold or warm water (squeezed)
- 1 cup honey or 1/2 cup agave (according to taste)
- 3 slivers of raw garlic
- 1/2 tbsp raw ginger (sliced)
- 1/2 tbsp ginger (ground)
- 1/4 tsp turmeric (ground)
- ½ - 1 tsp red pepper/cayenne pepper
- 1 tsp sea moss - optional)

NOTE:
Children only need a little of the tonic for it to become effective and suitable for their respiratory and immune systems. Start with ½ tsp pepper when creating this tonic recipe. If you desire more "heat," do not exceed 1 tsp pepper.
Gradually administer one teaspoon to your child once a week. For excessive inflammation, you can administer one teaspoon three (3) times a week, preferably every other day, not to exceed ½ cup.

READY TO MIX:
Mix the Base Ingredients in a large pitcher in the order listed and stir to ensure that flavors blend nicely. Let the ingredients sit for about 30 minutes. Taste Your Base. Strengthening your base ingredients is essential here, but remember that the tonic should have a bitter-sweet consistency. If you need more flavor, gradually add more.

Hibiscus Tonic

> This recipe is another immunity booster that helps to reduce inflammation. Hibiscus has several beneficial properties for the body, including lowering blood pressure, anti-oxidants, and improved heart and liver health, which benefits kidney functions.

INGREDIENTS
BASE:

- 8 cups hot water
- 7-10 slivers of raw ginger (based on taste and the type of bite you desire)
- 1 cup Hibiscus Tea (Grounded Bulk)
- 1-2 cups agave or desired sweetener (according to taste)
- 1 tbsp ginger (ground)
- 1/2 tsp turmeric (ground)
- 1 tsp sea moss - optional

NOTE:
This tonic is packed with immunity-boosting properties. Due to its potency, take one cup per week. If necessary, increase the frequency to three times a week.

READY TO MIX:
In a medium pot, put all of the ingredients on low heat in the order listed. Stir and let everything come to a slow boil to ensure the flavors blend nicely. Taste Your Base.

Strengthening your base ingredients is essential here. If you need more flavor, add more hibiscus, if you need more sweetener, add agave or whatever you desire. Let everything steep for about 30 minutes; then strain. Taste Your Base. Add if anything else is needed.

Mango Lassi

> This drink is a versatile companion, particularly delightful when paired with Asian or African-inspired dishes. Its refreshing coolness beautifully complements the heat and spices in these cuisines, creating a harmonious balance with each bite. Occasionally, I find myself savoring this drink alone as a liquid dessert. Can be a non-dairy treat also.

INGREDIENTS
BASE:
- 1 cup dahi, plain, goat milk yogurt or non-dairy option
- ½ cup goat milk or non-dairy option
- 2 tbsp brown sugar
- ½ tsp golden milk* (optional)
- 1/4 tsp anise* (ground) – optional
- ¼ tsp cinnamon* (ground) – optional
- ¼ tsp nutmeg* (ground) – optional
- ¼ tsp allspice* (ground) - optional

OTHER INGREDIENTS:
- 1 cup mangos (fresh or frozen chopped)
- ½ cup ice – optional

NOTE:
*Heavenly Golden Milk Recipe (See Beverages). If using, gradually add ½ tsp increments until you reach the desired flavor. If you are not using Heavenly Golden Milk, add Anise, Cinnamon, Allspice, or Nutmeg instead—the choice is yours.

READY TO MIX:
Prepare the Base Ingredients in the blender in the order listed and blend for a few minutes. Now, the most exciting part is to Taste Your Base. If you need to enhance the flavor, do so in small increments.

Then, add the mangoes and blend for a few more minutes. Again, Taste Your Base. If you need to enhance the flavor, do so in small increments. If you desire a smoother, creamy consistency, gradually add ice. The process of tasting and adjusting is where the magic happens! ENJOY!

SWEETS

Bread Pudding

I like to use everything because, as my dad used to say, "Nothing is to be Wasted." This recipe is a testament to that, offering a clever way to use up a few days-old bread, whether you baked it yourself or bought it from the store. It's a thrifty and resourceful approach that's sure to impress.

INGREDIENTS
BASE:

- 1 cup raisins
- 1 apple (finely minced)
- ¼ apple cider+
- ¼ cup of bourbon +
- 1 qt of goat or condensed milk
- 2 cups of brown sugar
- 2 tbsp vanilla extract*
- ¼ tsp allspice
- ¼ tsp cinnamon
- ¼ tsp nutmeg
- 3 tbsp butter (unsalted)
- ¼ tsp anise - optional

BOURBON SAUCE:

- 1 cup brown sugar
- ½ cup butter
- ¼ cup goat or evaporated milk
- Use soaked raisins, apple, cider, and/or bourbon sauce
- 1 egg

OTHER INGREDIENTS:

- 6-7 cups of bread (old) suggestions sourdough or French – cut in cubes
- 3 eggs (large)
- 1 tbsp butter (melted) for greasing pan

KITCHEN SINK:

*If you must use imitation vanilla, mix 4-5 teaspoons of agave or honey and 2-3 teaspoons of ground vanilla beans or vanilla powder in a small container.

BREAD PUDDING (CONTINUED)

Another option is to use Vanilla Bean Torani Syrup with one teaspoon of ground vanilla beans or powder with 1-2 teaspoons of agave or honey, according to taste. Mix thoroughly.

After letting it sit for about five (5) minutes, it's time to take control. Taste Your Base to ensure that you have the desired vanilla flavor. This step puts you in the driver's seat, giving you the confidence that your dish will turn out just right.

NOTE:
PREPARE EARLY - +Only mix raisins and apples with apple cider and/or bourbon in a medium bowl and let it soak for at least an hour to 1.5 hours. (Soaked Mixture)

READY TO MIX:
Don't worry, this recipe is flexible. Mix all the Base Ingredients together in a medium bowl in the order listed. To control the consistency of the mixture, you can use a hand whisker, but if not, a Nutri Bullet, blender, or food processor works just as well. Taste Your Base and relax, you're doing great.

Add 1/4 cup of the Soaked Mixture you prepared earlier to the base ingredients. Taste Your Base. If needed, add additional ingredients for the required taste.

Whip the 3 eggs separately, then gradually add them to the Base Ingredients. Next, add the bread to the Base Ingredients and thoroughly soak to ensure each piece absorbs the ingredients.

Heat the oven to 350 degrees. Greasing may not be necessary if using a glass pan. If not using a glass pan, use ½ tsp of melted butter and grease a 9x5-inch pan. Add the bread mixture to the pan and bake for 35 minutes. Allow it to sit in the oven after cutting it off for about 7-10 additional minutes.

BREAD PUDDING (CONTINUED)

While cooking the bread pudding, create the Bourbon Sauce. On low heat, add the sauce ingredients in the order listed (except for the egg) in a small pot, including the remaining Soaked Mixture you prepared earlier. Mix thoroughly as the mixture begins to thicken.

Continue mixing until a low simmer. Taste Your Base. Add additional ingredients if desired. Gradually add the egg slowly to avoid scrambling. Allow the sauce to set for 10-15 minutes.

Frequently check the cake using a toothpick. Stick the toothpick into the cake at different locations until the toothpick comes out clean. The bread should pull from the edges and get brown.

Let it cool for about 15 minutes, remove it from the pan, and cool for five more minutes. You can either spread the glaze over the bread or set it aside to use as needed. If you are spreading it over the cake, ensure it is completely cool before adding it.

Homemade Apple Pie

> Apple, peach, blueberry, or other pies, especially the filling, can be tricky to create. This homemade pie was fun to make, and I had to get creative to ensure the filling wasn't too loose and the apples were flavorful.

INGREDIENTS
BASE:

- 1 cup of brown sugar
- 3 tbsp butter (unsalted and melted)
- ½ cup hazelnut syrup (Torani)
- ¼ tsp allspice
- ¼ tsp cinnamon
- ¼ tsp nutmeg
- Pinch salt
- ¼ tsp anise - optional

OTHER INGREDIENTS:

- 4-5 medium apples (sliced)+
- ¼ cup flour
- 1 tsp cornstarch
- ½ cup water
- 9-inch pie crust shell
- Pie strips (lattice for top)

NOTE:
PREPARE EARLY - +Mix all Base Ingredients in the order listed and blend thoroughly. Taste Your Base. If you need additional ingredients, do so gradually to suit your taste.

HOMEMADE APPLE PIE (CONTINUED)

Place the apples in a medium bowl. Pour the Base Ingredient mixture over the apples, ensuring that each apple is thoroughly coated. Refrigerate the apple mixture overnight or for at least eight (8) hours.

Letting the apple mixture settle allows the flavors to soften and penetrate the apples. I usually use either Pink Lady or Honeycrisp Apples.

ANOTHER OPTION+:
1. Mix all Base Ingredients in the order listed and blend thoroughly in a medium saucepan on low heat;
2. Stir frequently to avoid sticking, and bring to a light boil;
3. Taste Your Base. If you want more flavors, gradually add them.

Gradually add your sliced apples to the Base Ingredients and stir thoroughly until you attain a light boil. This allows the apples to soften and the flavors to penetrate. I usually use Pink Lady or Honeycrisp Apples.

READY TO MIX:
If you use the Prepare Early recipe, take your Base Mixture from the refrigerator and put it in a medium saucepan on low heat. Stir frequently to avoid sticking, mix well, and bring to a light boil. Taste Your Base. If you want more flavors, gradually add them.

Remove the mixture from the heat and let it cool for both options. To add thickness, mix 1 tbsp flour with 1 tsp cornstarch in a small bowl if your filling is a little loose. Add this mixture to your filling, stir, and let it settle for about five minutes.

HOMEMADE APPLE PIE (CONTINUED)

Also, remember that once in the oven, the filling will solidify more due to the heat, so it is ideal to do this in increments of 1 tsp flour to ½ tsp cornstarch to acquire the desired thickness. Once it settles, you can determine if more dry ingredients must be added to your pie filling. Repeat only if required.

Set the oven to 400 degrees. Bake only the pie crust for about 2-3 minutes to brown it. Pour the filling mixture into the pie crust.

Cut the lattice strips to layer over the pie. Reduce the oven temperature to 385 degrees and bake the pie for 20 minutes, allowing the filling to settle and everything to blend thoroughly. Remove the pie from the oven and let it sit for about 5-10 minutes more, but ensure the crust doesn't burn.

Remove the pie from the oven and let it cool for 15 minutes. Enjoy!

NITA'S Buttermilk Lemony Loaf

I enjoy indulging in baked goods occasionally, and one of my go-to treats is my versatile buttermilk lemony loaf. This loaf strikes a perfect balance, being both light and sweet. It pairs wonderfully with a glass of milk, a scoop of ice cream, or simply on its own. And just like many of my recipes, you can freeze some batter for a later indulgence.

INGREDIENTS

BASE:
- 4 tbsp fresh (about 4-6 squeezed lemons) or concentrated lemon juice
- 1 1/2 tbsp fresh rind (finely ground) or 1 1/2 tbsp lemon extract
- 1/3 cup cream cheese (room temperature)
- 2 sticks of butter (melted and cooled) and ½ tsp butter to grease baking pan
- 4 eggs (room temperature)
- 1 cup brown sugar (packed)
- 1/2 tsp kosher or sea salt

DRY INGREDIENTS:
- 3/4 cup all-purpose flour
- 3/4 cup cake flour or Bisquick
- 1 tsp baking powder

GLAZE:
- 1 1/2 tbsp fresh lemon juice
- 1 1/2 tsp lemon extract
- 1 cup powdered sugar
- 1/2 cup heavy cream
- ½ cup buttermilk
- 1-2 tbsp cream cheese- optional for thickening

READY TO MIX:

Mix the Base Ingredients in the order listed (except the eggs and ½ tsp extra butter) in a medium bowl. Remember to Taste Your Base to ensure the perfect taste and consistency. This step is crucial and will give you the confidence that your loaf will turn out just right.

NITA'S BUTTERMILK LEMONY LOAF (CONTINUED)

Whip the eggs separately, then add them to the Base Ingredients. In a small bowl, mix Dry Ingredients thoroughly. Gradually add Base Ingredients to the Dry Ingredients until thoroughly blended.

Heat the oven to 350 degrees. Use the ½ tsp melted butter to grease a 9x5-inch pan and pour the ingredients into the pan. Bake for about 40-45 minutes and let it sit in the oven for 10-15 minutes.

Use a toothpick to stick it into different locations to ensure it is ready. If the pick comes out clean, the cake is ready; if not, let it sit in the oven for a few more minutes. While the cake's cooking, create the glaze.

In a small bowl, add the glaze ingredients in the order listed. Mix with a hand whisk to control consistency. Taste Your Base.

If you want a thicker glaze, gradually add cream cheese or water for a thinner glaze. Whichever you choose, do so gradually. Remove the cake from the oven and let it cool for about 15 minutes, then remove it from the pan and let it cool for 5 minutes.

Once the cake has completely cooled, gradually add the glaze. Allow 10-15 minutes to set before slicing and serving. Refrigerate and wrap properly. While refrigerated, the cake will last for about 3-5 days.

Oatmeal Spice Cookies

Now and then, I want a nice, simple treat; this is one of our favorites. Sometimes, I want a more flavorful cookie so that I may add a few options to the recipe. Take the liberty to do the same for yourself.

INGREDIENTS:
BASE:

- 2 cups brown sugar (packed)
- 2 sticks of butter = 1 cup (melted)
- 1 tsp nutmeg
- 1 tsp allspice
- 1 tsp cinnamon
- 2 tsp real vanilla extract*
- 2 eggs
- ¼ tsp anise - optional
- ¼ cup liquid hazelnut - optional**

DRY INGREDIENTS:

- 4 cups oatmeal***
- 1 1/2 cups flour+
- 1/2 cup and 2 tbsp wheat flour+
- 1/4 tsp baking powder
- 1 1/3 tsp kosher or sea salt
- 1 tbsp flaxseed - optional
- 1/2 cup cranberries - optional
- 1/2 cup shredded coconut - optional
- ½ cup pecan pieces - optional

KITCHEN SINK:

*If you must use imitation vanilla, mix 4-5 teaspoons of agave or honey and 2-3 teaspoons of ground vanilla beans or vanilla powder in a small container. Another option is to use Vanilla Bean Torani Syrup with one teaspoon of ground vanilla beans or powder with 1-2 teaspoons of agave or honey, according to taste. Mix thoroughly.

OATMEL SPICE COOKIES (CONTINUED)

After letting it sit for about five (5) minutes, it's time to take control. Taste Your Base to ensure that you have the desired vanilla flavor. This step puts you in the driver's seat, giving you the confidence that your dish will turn out just right.

**Besides adding vanilla extract, you can boost the flavors by adding liquid hazelnut or your favorite liqueur syrup. Torani is my favorite, but you can use any brand.
*** You can leave your oats whole or put them in a blender and pulse for a few minutes to create a more chopped-up oat.

+ If you want to avoid using wheat flour, regular flour also works in the total amount suggested

NOTE:
You can save some of this batch later by rolling it in plastic cling wrap and freezing it. When ready to eat, please remove it from the freezer, unwrap it, cut off slices, and bake.

Here are some options for preparing them, especially if you want crispy cookies:
1) If you just made the batch, flatten and shape them and then place them in the oven. 2) If they've been in the freezer, take them out for about five (5) minutes before baking and flatten them before placing them in the oven. 3) If you just got them out of the freezer and want to bake them immediately instead of waiting for five (5) minutes, place them in the oven, but after two (2) minutes, flatten them.

OATMEL SPICE COOKIES (CONTINUED)

READY TO MIX

Mix the base ingredients thoroughly, including the options, except for the eggs, in a medium bowl. To make the job easier, use a fork or a hand whisker. Beat until creamy. Taste Your Base.

Gradually add more ingredients if needed for the desired flavor. Next, add the eggs and continue mixing thoroughly. Set aside.

Mix the Dry Ingredients in a medium bowl in the order above, including the options if you desire. Make sure that the ingredients are thoroughly mixed together. Gradually add the Base Ingredients to the Dry Ingredients and stir frequently to ensure all ingredients blend.

Set aside for about 5 minutes. Using your hands, teaspoons or tablespoons, measure the size of the cookies and place them on a cast iron skillet or cookie sheet.

Using an Air Fryer is a breeze for this recipe. Bake your cookies at 385 degrees for 6 minutes. The outside may seem cooked and brown, but not the inside. Let the cookies settle for a few minutes.

Another option is to preheat the oven to 385 degrees and bake for 7-10 minutes. To achieve crispier cookies, turn off the oven. Let the cookies sit in the oven for a few minutes, then remove them. For those who prefer softer cookies, bake for 5 minutes, then remove from the oven. Let them settle, and rest assured—they'll be perfect for your enjoyment.

Pineapple Upside-Down Cake

I love pineapples, and this is one of my favorite treats. I enjoy almost everything pineapple from ice cream sherbert to cake. I've created just the right balance of sweetness; also, in this recipe, I've provided an option that you may enjoy adding to your cake.

INGREDIENTS:
BASE:

- 1 cup brown sugar
- ¼ cup powdered sugar
- 10 tbsp butter (melted and unsalted) = 2/3 cups or 1 1/3 sticks
- ½ tsp vanilla extract*
- ½ cup sour cream
- ½ cup plain yogurt
- Pineapple juice from 20 oz can (approximately 1/3 cup remains)
- 2 eggs
- ¼ cup coconut flakes - optional

OTHER INGREDIENTS:

- 1 ¼ cup all-purpose flour
- 1 ¼ tsp baking powder
- ¼ tsp kosher salt
- 20 oz can pineapples (approximately 10 slices)

KITCHEN SINK:

*If you must use imitation vanilla, mix 4-5 teaspoons of agave or honey and 2-3 teaspoons of ground vanilla beans or vanilla powder in a small container. Another option is to use Vanilla Bean Torani Syrup with one teaspoon of ground vanilla beans or powder with 1-2 teaspoons of agave or honey, according to taste. Mix thoroughly.

PINEAPPLE UPSIDE DOWN CAKE (CONTINUED)

After letting it sit for about five (5) minutes, it's time to take control. Taste Your Base to ensure that you have the desired vanilla flavor. This step puts you in the driver's seat, giving you the confidence that your dish will turn out just right.

READY TO MIX:
Mix the Base Ingredients thoroughly in the order listed (except the eggs), including the pineapple juice and the option if you choose, in a medium bowl. Taste Your Base. Add additional ingredients gradually if needed for the desired taste.

Mix the flour, salt, and baking powder in another medium bowl, stirring thoroughly before adding them to the Base Ingredients. Gradually add eggs to the Base Ingredients. To control the consistency of the mixture, you can use a hand whisker, but if not, a NutriBullet, blender, or food processor works.

Cover the bottom of a medium pan with the pineapples and pour the mixture over it. Heat the oven to 375 degrees. Bake for about 40 minutes.

Cut off the oven and allow the cake to settle in for about 15 minutes. Frequently check the cake using a toothpick, sticking it in different locations. If it doesn't come out clean, let it sit in the oven for about five (5) more minutes.

Once the toothpick comes out clean, it's ready. Remove from the oven and cool for about 20-30 minutes. Enjoy with ice cream, gelato, milk, or alone.

Spice Granola Mix

> You can create this delicious spice granola mix by altering the oatmeal cookie recipe. Have fun with creating your granola and add what you desire with moderation from cranberries, coconut flakes, flaxseeds, and pecans to pumpkin seeds. If you are like me, you can make this mix as a quick snack to eat alone, add it to your favorite desserts, such as ice cream and yogurt, or eat it as cereal. Just as with the oatmeal cookie recipe, you can wrap, freeze, and bake to use for later.

INGREDIENTS:
BASE:

- 2 cups brown sugar (packed)
- 2 sticks of butter (1 cup, melted)
- 1 tsp nutmeg
- 1 tsp allspice
- 1 tsp cinnamon
- 2 tsp real vanilla extract*
- 2 eggs
- ¼ tsp anise - optional
- ¼ cup liquid hazelnut - optional**

DRY INGREDIENTS:

- 4 cups oatmeal***
- 1 1/2 cups flour+
- 1/2 cup and 2 tbsp wheat flour+
- 1/4 tsp baking powder
- 1 1/3 tsp kosher or sea salt

KITCHEN SINK:

*If you must use imitation vanilla, mix 4-5 teaspoons of agave or honey and 2-3 teaspoons of ground vanilla beans or vanilla powder in a small container. Another option is to use Vanilla Bean Torani Syrup with one teaspoon of ground vanilla beans or powder with 1-2 teaspoons of agave or honey, according to taste. Mix thoroughly.

SPICE GRANOLA MIX (CONTINUED)

After letting it sit for about five (5) minutes, it's time to take control. Taste Your Base to ensure that you have the desired vanilla flavor. This step puts you in the driver's seat, giving you the confidence that your dish will turn out just right.

**Besides adding vanilla extract, you can boost the flavors by adding liquid hazelnut or your favorite liqueur syrup. Torani is my favorite, but you can use any brand.
*** You can leave your oats whole or put them in a blender and pulse for a few minutes to create a more chopped-up oat.

+ If you want to avoid using wheat flour, regular flour also works in the total amount suggested.

NOTE:
You can save some of this batch later by rolling it in plastic cling wrap and freezing it. When ready to eat, please remove it from the freezer, unwrap it, cut off slices, and bake.

Here are some options for preparing them: 1) If you just made the batch, flatten and shape them and then place them in the oven. 2) If they've been in the freezer, take them out for about five (5) minutes before baking and flatten them before placing them in the oven. 3) If you just got them out of the freezer and want to bake them immediately instead of waiting for five (5) minutes, place them in the oven, but after two (2) minutes, flatten them.

Consider adding whatever you want to your granola mix from coconut flakes, flaxseeds, pumpkin seeds, cranberries, raisins, pecan, or almonds the choice is your but do so gradually to not overpower the mixture and to cook thoroughly.

SPICE GRANOLA MIX (CONTINUED)

READY TO MIX:

Mix the base ingredients thoroughly, including the options, except for the eggs, in a medium bowl. To make the job easier, use a fork or a hand whisker. Beat until creamy. Taste Your Base.

Gradually add more ingredients if needed for the desired flavor. Next, add the eggs and continue mixing thoroughly. Set aside.

Mix the Dry Ingredients in a medium bowl in the order above, including the options if you desire. Make sure that the ingredients are thoroughly mixed together. Gradually add the Base Ingredients to the Dry Ingredients and stir frequently to ensure all ingredients blend.

Set aside for about 5 minutes. An Air Fryer would not be advisable for this recipe. Regardless of the option that you choose under the Note, the remaining process is the same.

Put 10 slices (if frozen or refrigerated) or scoops (if freshly made) of the mixture and place on the cast iron skillet or cookie sheet. Preheat the oven to 400 degrees and bake for ten minutes. At the five-minute interval, using a wooden spoon, flatten, agitate, and smash the cookie mixture.

This is the step for creating the perfect granola texture. Cut off the oven, agitate the mixture more, then spread the granola across the pan and let it settle in the oven for a few minutes. Continue watching the granola to avoid burning. Remove, cool, and enjoy!

HOW TO USE BRINE, RUBS, & SAUCES

Brine, rubs, or sauces added to your meats create a beautiful note, flavor, and texture. Also, marinating the meat cuts the cooking time yet leaves your meat tender. In addition to what each Recipe requires, consider these steps as a part of your process as well:

1. Create your base as suggested, along with your choice of fresh or dried herbs and no salt unless otherwise required. You don't want the salt to compete with the base ingredients.

2. Combine everything in a medium bowl and let it sit for at least 45-60 minutes to infuse all the flavors before adding them to the meat. Taste Your Base to determine if the flavor suits your needs. If more flavor is needed, gradually add the base ingredients until you reach the desired flavors.

3. If you desire, you can lightly cut some slits into the meat so that the base ingredients can infuse into the meat. Pour the base ingredients over the meat and thoroughly massage. Let the meat and flavors set and infuse for at least 8 hours or overnight for a more robust flavor. Turn the meat over every few hours so the base can infuse adequately.

4. After marinating in the base ingredients, you can choose from several options when cooking your meat; the choice is yours. Here are some options:
- a) Place beef, lamb, or goat directly in the oven at 385 degrees for 30 minutes and chicken at 375 degrees for 20 minutes or as you prefer, or
- b) Use a grill or smoker; or
- c) Crock Pot (except for poultry)+ on low for a few hours; or
- d) You can sear your meat turning it over after about 5-7 minutes on medium heat creating caramelized skin, yet the inside remains juicy.

HOW TO USE BRINE, RUBS, & SAUCES (CONTINUED)

NOTE:

Try our Japanese Steakhouse Restaurant Ginger Sauce (See Recipe) if you want a spicier, more robust flavor. Use only 1/2 cup of the Ginger Sauce. The amount of Ginger Sauce you use is determined by the size of the meat.

The Ginger Sauce provides a unique flavor profile that can elevate your dish. I usually create more sauce and freeze or refrigerate it for later use. See the full Recipe for more details.

Maximize the practicality of your kitchen by repurposing small glass containers for storing brine in the refrigerator or for dry rubs conveniently placed in your pantry. Use the brine, sauces, or rubs within 90-120 days. Occasionally, the ingredients may separate, but a simple shake of the container will continue to blend the flavors.

+ Another option for people who do not wish to use a Crock Pot is a Dutch Pot. If you do not have either, use what you have. The idea is to ensure the ingredients infuse the meat and cook all around it thoroughly.
++ You can substitute placing the poultry in the cast iron or flat plate for placing it in a skillet on the stove, turning it over, and lightly searing it on low heat for about 10-15 minutes. Remember to be patient with the process while carefully watching your meat.

Brine

This brine is ideal for all types of meat. The amount of brine needed depends upon the size of the meat prepared. Use this brine for approximately 10 lbs; however, reduce or increase the base ingredients to half or more accordingly. For chicken, add the additional ingredients as stated.

INGREDIENTS:
BASE:

- 2 cups soy sauce, amino acids, or tamari*
- 2 cups vinegar (white or apple cider)
- 1/4 tsp turmeric (powder)
- 1/4 tsp ginger (powder)
- 7-10 cloves garlic (sliced)
- 1 tbsp garlic powder (use for poultry only)
- 1 tbsp onion powder (use for poultry only)
- 1/2 cup green onion (chopped)
- 1/2 cup white onion (minced)
- 1/2 cup brown sugar

SUGGESTED HERBS: *Preferably Fresh*

- thyme
- rosemary
- oregano
- basil
- cilantro

3-4 sprigs of each chosen fresh herb. Either remove leaves from sprigs or use whole sprigs. If you are using dried, bottled, or packaged seasonings, use 1-2 tsp each of the ideal suggested herbs noted above.

KITCHEN SINK:
*For the different flavors of soy sauce, amino acid, and tamari, go to What Flavor Suits You? under the Helpful Hints section.

READY TO MIX:
Refer to the Using The Brine, Rubs, & Sauces section for how to use it effectively.

Japanese Ginger Sauce

> This sauce is a versatile condiment, perfect for quick kitchen fixes. Whether adding a hint of flavor to a salad, marinating meat or enhancing the taste of your favorite side dish, this sauce should be your go-to. The amount of sauce you use and its purpose can vary depending on the dish or meat size, so feel free to experiment.
>
> Remember, the base below is ideal if the meat size is approximately 10 lbs; however, if less or more meat is needed, reduce or increase as needed.

INGREDIENTS:
BASE:

- 2 cups tamari, soy sauce, or amino acid*
- 2 cups rice vinegar
- 2 tbsp powdered ginger or 1/2 cup fresh ginger (sliced)
- 3 cloves garlic (sliced)
- 1 cup brown sugar
- 1/2 cup red onion (sliced)
- • 1 tbsp lemon juice

KITCHEN SINK:
*For the different flavors of soy sauce, amino acid, and tamari, go to What Flavor Suits You? under the Helpful Hints section.

READY TO MIX:
Refer to the Using The Brine, Rubs, & Sauces section for how to use it effectively.

Meat Rub

INGREDIENTS:
BASE:

- 4 tbsp garlic (powder)
- 4 tbsp onion (powder)
- 4 tbsp kosher salt
- 2 tbsp paprika
- 1 ½ tbsp curry
- 1 tbsp rosemary (ground)
- 1 tbsp turmeric
- 1 tbsp ginger (ground)
- 1 tbsp ground allspice
- 2 tsp cumin
- 1 tsp coriander
- 1 tsp nutmeg
- 1 tsp cinnamon (ground)
- 1 tsp lemon pepper
- 1 tsp ground pepper
- 2 tbsp creole seasoning – spicy optional

This meat rub is an excellent hack for adding beautiful flavors to your meat and getting it right each time. I create this mixture and store it in a repurposed glass container like I do many of my other herbs and spices in the pantry. It is suitable for at least 90-120 days.

SUGGESTED HERBS: *Ground Preferred*
- thyme
- basil
- cilantro
- Rosemary
- oregano

READY TO MIX:
Refer to the Using The Brine, Rubs, & Sauces section for how to use it effectively.

Nita's Nibble Rub

There are times when I need to cook a meal quickly and want to take as many shortcuts as possible. This rub allows me to quickly and easily apply it to any meat. The ingredients below make about ½ - 1 cup of rub, ideal for up to 7-10 lbs of meat.

If you want to use it for more meat, I suggest that you double the ingredients. This rub is less spicy than the other one but has a kick. I create this mixture and store it in a repurposed glass container like I do many of my other herbs and spices in the pantry. It is suitable for at least 90- 120 days.

INGREDIENTS:
BASE:

- 1 tbsp onion (minced or powder)
- 1 tbsp garlic (powder)
- 1 tsp chili powder
- 1 tbsp turmeric
- 1 tbsp curry
- 1 tbsp paprika
- 1 tbsp ginger (powder)
- 1 tsp cumin
- 1 tsp coriander
- 1 tsp basil
- 1 tbsp lemon pepper
- 1 tsp rosemary (powder)
- 4 tbsp kosher salt (if less than 10 lbs, reduce by half)

READY TO MIX:
Refer to the Using The Brine, Rubs, & Sauces section for how to use it effectively.

Nita's Nibble Rub — SPICY!

I choose this rub for those quick meals when I want it a bit spicy. It is similar to the other rub, but this one has more kick. This rub allows me to quickly and easily apply it to any meat. The ingredients below make about ½ - 1 cup of rub, ideal for up to 7-10 lbs of meat.

If you want to use it for more meat, I suggest that you double the ingredients. Sometimes, I create enough of this rub for just one meal or enough to store in a repurposed glass container and put it in the pantry. If you desire to store some of it, it is suitable for at least 90-120 days in an airtight container.

INGREDIENTS:
BASE:

- 1 tbsp onion (minced or powder)
- 1 tbsp garlic (powder)
- 1 tbsp turmeric
- 1 tsp cumin
- 1 tsp coriander
- 1 tbsp curry
- 1 tbsp ginger (powder)
- 1 tsp basil
- 1 tbsp lemon pepper
- 1 tsp rosemary (powder)
- 3 tbsp kosher salt (if less than 10 lbs, reduce the salt by half)
- 1 tsp cayenne pepper or crushed pepper (depending upon the desired heat – cayenne is much hotter than crushed pepper)

READY TO MIX:
Refer to the Using The Brine, Rubs, & Sauces section for how to use it effectively.

STARTERS

Artichoke & Spinach
DIP & SPREAD

Everyone loves a good snack now and then. Why not choose a snack that is not only flavorful but when you decide to cheat either from a diet or on a late-night one that you would enjoy? You can substitute the cheeses with vegan versions to make this dish less fattening yet still delicious.

Enjoy this dish as a flavorful dip or spread on your favorite baguette, sourdough bread, or tortilla chip.

INGREDIENTS:
BASE:

- 3 tbsp Mayonnaise
- 1/2 cup Sour Cream*
- 1/4 cup or 4 oz. Neufchâtel Cheese or Cream Cheese*
- 1/2 cup heavy whipping cream
- 1/4 cup Mozzarella Cheese*
- 1/4 cup Cheddar Cheese*
- 1/4 cup Regular Parmesan Cheese*
- 1 tbsp Nutritional Yeast
- 1/2 tsp Sea or Kosher Salt
- 1/4 tsp Black Pepper
- 2 tbsp olive oil
- 1 Red or White Onion (diced)
- 3 Cloves Garlic (finely diced)
- 1 Red Bell Pepper (diced)
- 1 tbsp Sea Moss - optional

OTHER INGREDIENTS:
- 10 oz package artichoke hearts (frozen, thawed, rinsed, and patted dry)
- 1 1/2 handfuls fresh spinach or 10 oz spinach (frozen. thawed, rinsed, and patted dry.

KITCHEN SINK:
*You can substitute the cheeses or sour cream with vegan products.

ARTICHOKE & SPINACH DIP & SPREAD (CONTINUED)

NOTE:
+Blend the ingredients if you want a spread (purée consistency). Gradually pulse for a dip (chunky consistency). Continue to blend or pulse the ingredients until you reach the desired consistency. See below.

READY TO MIX:
Preheat oven to 375 degrees.

Mix all base ingredients in a medium-sized mixing bowl, including sea moss if you are using it, except for olive oil, onion, garlic, and pepper. Stir thoroughly and let the ingredients sit for about ten minutes. Taste Your Base.

In a large skillet, sauté onion, garlic, and bell pepper with olive oil for about 20-30 seconds. Then add hearts and spinach and sautee for 1-3 minutes, blending all ingredients thoroughly. Place this mixture, including the base ingredients, in a blender, food processor, or bullet and either pulsate or blend all ingredients.+ Let everything sit for ten minutes. Taste Your Base.

If you desire, you can gradually add additional ingredients according to taste. If you want more spice, add garlic. For a creamier consistency, you can use either sour or cream cheese. Looking for more salt, go for it. Taste Your Base. Get creative with this dish, whether you're preparing it as a dip or spread.

As you add ingredients, Taste Your Base. Allow time to settle before adding additional ingredients to avoid overwhelming the flavors. Next, place the blended or pulsated ingredients in a baking pan or dish and bake for 10-15 minutes. Cut off the oven and let it sit for 10 minutes so the ingredients can settle. Enjoy!

Baked Potato Soup

Sometimes, you want to create a dish that gives you warmth. If you are looking for some quick comfort, try this dish. It wraps you up and provides everything you need, especially on those quick-fix or cold days.

INGREDIENTS:
BASE:
- 1 1/3 cups coconut milk*
- 2 cups heavy cream or evaporated milk*
- 4 (8 oz) cans or 3 (12 oz) cans Chicken Broth or ½ cup boullion**
- 1 cup Beef Broth or ½ cup boullion**
- 5 cups of water (depending upon taste)
- ½ stick butter
- 1/4 tsp turmeric (powder)
- ¼ tsp ginger (powder)
- ½ tsp black pepper
- 1 ¼ cups pepper jack, Havarti or cheddar cheese (shredded)
- 2 tbsp all-purpose flour or 1 tsp sea moss (optional) (used to add thickness)

OTHER INGREDIENTS:
- 2 sprigs fresh dill (finely chopped)
- 1.5 tsp each spice (fresh powder or finely chopped):
    - o Basil
    - o Oregano
    - o Parsley
    - o Lavender
- 1/8 to ½ tsp Cayenne pepper, crushed pepper or paprika*** (based upon taste)
- 3 large white or purple sweet potato or yam or 10 small red potatoes (chopped)
- 2 clove garlic (minced)
- 2 tbsp red onion (minced)
- 1 green onion (minced)
- 4-6 slices of crispy bacon (beef or pork)

BAKED POTATO SOUP (CONTINUED)

KITCHEN SINK:
If you have vegetables like corn or carrots, you can add them to your baked potatoes medley. You can either keep them whole or finely chopped.

NOTE:
*Low-fat option is to substitute the heavy cream or evaporated milk with more coconut milk to reduce your dairy intake. If you use the substitution, reduce the total water intake by 1 cup.

**Bouillon is preferred for this dish because it allows you to control the taste. Canned broths will not negate the flavors, but you may have to add salt. If you do not use the bouillon but instead broth, reduce the total water intake by 1 cup.

***The crushed or cayenne peppers boost the other flavors; be mindful of how much pepper you use. If you don't like spicy food, use paprika instead. Either way, you will still be able to experience a flavorful dish.

Purple sweet potato or yam will give your dish a slightly sweet taste but not overpowering. It provides many more healthy benefits than a white potato, from blood sugar control to improved digestion, boosting dietary fiber, and reducing inflammation but it has an acquired taste.

READY TO MIX:
Thoroughly clean potatoes and place them in a heated oven at 400 degrees for about 50-60 minutes. To check potato readiness, prick with a toothpick. The potatoes are ready if the pick comes out clean and easy—cool, peel, and chop.

BAKED POTATO SOUP (CONTINUED)

Put the bacon in the oven at the same time. After it is crispy and thoroughly cooked, remove it and cool. Crumble the bacon.

Put all base ingredients in a medium pot in the order listed and stir thoroughly. Bring to a low boil. Taste Your Base. Gradually add additional ingredients if needed.

In a large pot, saute the onions and garlic with bacon grease. Add this mixture to the base ingredients, then add the spices, dill, and pepper. Stir thoroughly, add the baked potatoes, and bring everything to a medium boil.

You can now add vegetables like corn or carrots to the base ingredients. Add no more than one cup of vegetables to avoid overpowering the dish. Let everything settle for 7-10 minutes.

Taste Your Base. Gradually add additional ingredients if needed for flavor. Add bacon crumbles to the soup and stir thoroughly, or top off the soup with the bacon crumbles. At this point, it's crucial to Taste Your Base.

Broccoli Bake

> When people taste this dish, it reminds them of their favorite quiche, broccoli, or spinach casserole, depending upon their culture. No matter what culture or ethnicity we are related to, most dishes cross cultural lines in many ways. I see this dish as a marriage between vegetables and Mac and Cheese.

INGREDIENTS:

BASE:

- 1 can (10.5 oz) Campbell's Cream of Mushroom Soup
- 1 (10.5 oz) Velveeta Original Cheese Loaf*
- 5 cloves garlic (minced)
- 1 cup green onion (finely chopped)
- ½ tsp olive oil
- ½ cup Sea Moss (optional)**

OTHER INGREDIENTS:

- 2 cups white rice
- ½ tsp salt
- ½ tsp butter***
- 4 cups broccoli (chopped)

KITCHEN SINK:

Campbell's Cream of Mushroom has a robust and balanced flavor. You can use any brand, but depending on your preferred taste, you may need to add more seasoning to enhance the flavors.

BROCCOLI BAKE (CONTINUED)

*Instead of using the Velveeta Original Cheese Loaf, you can substitute it with your Favorite Cheese Spread, or you can use a few slices of the following:
- Swiss
- Cheddar
- Colby
- Pepper Jack
- Havarti

If you desire a more cheesy texture, add only five to seven slices to the base mix to create the right balance. Remember that the cheese and other ingredients will be added to the mushroom soup.

**Sea Moss will add thickness to the dish. It has no taste and absorbs whatever it touches, but as previously mentioned, it also has several nutrients. Try it; you will enjoy it!

***I prefer goat products for all my dishes due to their nutrients and health benefits, from butter and milk to cheeses. However, the milk is an acquired taste.

READY TO MIX:
In a small skillet, saute green onion and garlic with ½ tsp olive oil on medium heat for 30-45 seconds until translucent but not burnt. Set aside. Add the soup and Velveeta Loaf (or cheese substitute) to the onion and garlic mixture in a medium pot, including sea moss, if you are using it.

Stir everything thoroughly until all ingredients have blended into a smooth consistency. Let the base sit for 30 minutes to infuse all the flavors. Taste Your Base.

BROCCOLI BAKE (CONTINUED)

Prep rice as mentioned in the Properly Clean Your Food Before You Cook Section, your regular way or as directed on the package. Add 2 cups of water, ½ teaspoon salt, and ½ teaspoon butter to a small pot. Allow the water to boil, then add 2 cups of rice.

Stir thoroughly. After a second boil, remove the pot from the fire and cover with a lid. Set aside.

In a medium pot, add 2 cups of water in a medium pot with ½ teaspoon salt. Bring to a boil, and then add the broccoli. Cook until broccoli is still somewhat firm.

Drain and set aside. Set the oven to 380 degrees. Add one layer of rice and then one layer of broccoli mixture to a baking pan. Pour the base mixture over the rice and broccoli.

Repeat the rice and broccoli layers, adding the base mixture until all ingredients are gone. Allow about ½ inches empty from the top of the pan because the base mixture tends to boil over a little as it cooks. Puncture a few holes into the casserole to allow all ingredients to fuse throughout the pan.

butternut squash

As cold weather sets in, warming your body and gut is crucial. Your gut, the command center of your body, is vital in maintaining overall health. Warm foods, like butternut squash soup, are smart choices and are easier for your body to process, unlike cold foods, which require more energy to warm up.

INGREDIENTS:
BASE:

- 3-4 (14.5 oz cans) Chicken Broth or 2 teaspoons Chicken Bouillon*
- 3-4 (14.5 oz cans) Beef Broth or 2 teaspoon Beef Bouillon*
- 5 cups Water or more (depending upon taste)*
- 2.5 cups Heavy Whipping Cream**
- 1/2 cup coconut milk**
- 1/2 tsp jalapeño juice
- ½ tsp cinnamon
- ½ tsp coriander
- ½ tsp black pepper
- 1 tsp turmeric
- 1 tbsp Olive Oil
- 1 tsp crushed red pepper***
- 1 tsp paprika***
- 1 tsp cumin
- 1 tsp onion powder
- 1 tsp garlic powder
- 1 tsp ginger powder
- 1 tbsp sea moss (optional)

HERBS & SPICES

- 1/2 tsp ginger (finely chopped)
- 1/2 tsp dried or 1 sprig fresh basil
- 1/2 tsp or 1 sprig of rosemary
- 1/2 tsp dried oregano
- 1/2 tsp dried or fresh thyme
- 2-4 Bay Leaves

BUTTERNUT SQUASH (CONTINUED)

VEGETABLES:

- 1 tbsp garlic (minced) or 1 1/2 cloves (finely diced)
- 1 cup carrots (chopped or small carrots) = 1-2 carrots or ½ bag (shredded)
- 1 medium (russet white or purple sweet potato or yam) add thickness
- 1 medium sweet potato (chopped) or 3 small white potatoes (adds thickness)
- 1 cup onion (finely chopped)
- 1 cup celery (finely chopped)
- 1-2 sweet peppers (chopped)
- 1 medium butternut squash (chopped)

KITCHEN SINK:

Embrace the freedom to experiment with a variety of vegetables. You have the power to add almost any vegetable you have at home but remember to do so mindfully. Your goal is to enhance the dish's integrity without compromising its essence.

When trying new combinations, it's important to be mindful of overpowering flavors like celery or squash. This awareness will help you make informed decisions and discover the best flavor combinations for your dish. For instance, I found that adding a few mushrooms to mine one day was an awesome addition.

I have considered adding peanuts one day when I feel like being more adventurous. Get creative with this dish.

NOTE:

*Low-fat option is to substitute the heavy cream or evaporated milk with more coconut milk to reduce your dairy intake. If you use the substitution, reduce the total water intake by 1 cup.

BUTTERNUT SQUASH (CONTINUED)

NOTE (CONTINUED)
**Bouillon is preferred for this dish because it allows you to control the taste. Canned broths will not negate the flavors, but you may have to add salt. If you do not use the bouillon, reduce the total water intake by 1 cup.

***The crushed or cayenne peppers and paprika boost the other flavors and add heat; be mindful of how much you use.

Purple sweet potato or yam will give your dish a slightly sweet taste but not overpowering. It provides many more healthy benefits than a white potato, from blood sugar control to improved digestion, boosting dietary fiber, and reducing inflammation but an acquired taste.

READY TO MIX:
In a skillet, sauté the garlic, ginger, and onions with one tablespoon of olive oil for five seconds n low heat until translucent. While cooking, gradually add the herbs and spices and blend thoroughly for about ten to fifteen seconds.

Set the oven to 385 degrees and cook potatoes and squash for 45-60 minutes. Test the potatoes and squash by pricking a toothpick in their center. If it comes out clean and easy, the vegetables are ready, but if not, allow them to cook for about five more minutes.

Peel and chop the potatoes and squash. Next, add all the vegetables, except potatoes and squash, to the herb and spice mixture. Blend thoroughly. Add the Base Ingredients to a large pot on low heat. Stir thoroughly for about 10-15

BUTTERNUT SQUASH (CONTINUED)

minutes to avoid sticking. Bring to a light boil. Let everything settle for about 15-20 minutes. Taste Your Base. At this point, you should know how your soup will taste overall. Are you satisfied with the taste, or must you add something else?

If you desire to add more flavors, do so gradually, and then cook for about ten more minutes. Remove the soup from the stove and let it settle for about 15 minutes. Transfer your herbs, spices, and vegetables to the blender along with 1/2 cup of water and pulsate for 30-60 seconds. Add more water if needed to create a smooth consistency. After blending and reaching the desired consistency, put it into a pot on low heat.

Stir thoroughly and gradually add your Base Ingredients. Continue to stir to avoid sticking for about 20 more minutes. Taste Your Base. Gradually add more flavors if needed. Next, add your potatoes and squash. As the mixture continues to cook and break down, it will transform into a rich, creamy soup. Continue to cook slowly or blend again to reach your desired texture. Taste Your Base and add additional ingredients as needed. Enjoy your delicious butternut squash soup.

Corn Chowder Soup

Prepare this soup on chilly days or when you crave comfort foods. It's a nourishing dish that will give you a warm, secure feeling. Most importantly, enjoy the process of creating this comforting meal. It's not just about the result but the journey to get there.

INGREDIENTS:
BASE:

- 4 (8 oz) cans or 3 (12 oz) cans Chicken Broth or ½ cup Chicken bouillon*
- 5 cups of water or more (depending upon taste)*
- 1 ¾ cups coconut milk**
- 2 cups Whipping Heavy Cream**
- 1/4 tsp cayenne pepper or paprika***
- 1 tsp turmeric
- 2 tbsp Olive Oil
- 2 tsp sea or kosher salt
- 1/2 tsp dried or fresh oregano
- 2-4 Bay Leaves (finely chopped)
- 1/2 tsp dried or fresh thyme (finely chopped)
- 2 tbsp dried or fresh rosemary (finely chopped)
- 2 tbsp Chives (finely chopped)
- Pinch black pepper

OTHER INGREDIENTS:

- 1 tbsp garlic (minced) or 1 1/2 cloves (finely chopped)
- 1/2 cup white onion and 1/2 cup red onion (finely chopped)
- 1 cup carrots (chopped, small, or shredded)
- 2 cups (red, white or purple sweet) potatoes or yam peeled and chopped
- 3 stalks green onion (finely chopped)
- 1 cup celery (finely chopped)
- 2 (8 oz) or 1 (15.25 oz) can) or 6-7 ears (off the cob) corn
- 4 slices beef Bacon (crumbled)
- 1/4 - 1/2 cup of rice (optional)

CORN CHOWDER SOUP (CONTINUED)

NOTE:
*Bouillon is preferred for this dish because it allows you to control the taste. Canned broths will not negate the flavors, but you may have to add salt. If you do not use the bouillon, reduce the total water intake by 1 cup.

**A low-fat option is to substitute heavy cream or evaporated milk with more coconut milk to reduce dairy intake. If you use this substitution, reduce the total water intake by 1 cup.

***The crushed or cayenne peppers boost the other flavors; be mindful of how much pepper you use. If you don't like spicy food, use paprika instead. Either way, you will still be able to experience a flavorful dish.

Purple sweet potato or yam will give your dish a slightly sweet taste but not overpowering. It provides many more healthy benefits than a white potato, from blood sugar control to improved digestion, boosting dietary fiber, and reducing inflammation but an acquired taste.

READY TO MIX:
Start by blending the Base Ingredients in the order listed in a medium skillet on low heat, including 1 tbsp olive oil and ½ tsp salt. Stir thoroughly and bring to a light boil. Let it sit for about 5-7 minutes.

Tasting Your Base is crucial as it allows you to adjust the flavors to your liking. Adjust the ingredients as you go to ensure the soup meets your taste preferences.

Cook bacon in a medium skillet or the oven at 400 degrees until crisp. Place in a paper towel to remove the excess oil.

CORN CHOWDER SOUP (CONTINUED)

If you're cooking corn on the cob, add just enough water to cover the corn in a pot. Then, add 1 tbsp of olive oil and 1/2 tsp of salt, cook at a medium temperature, and bring to a boil. Drain the water, let the corn cool, and cut the kernels off the cob.

If using corn in a can, add 1 tbsp olive oil, ½ tsp salt, and corn in a small pot. Bring to a light boil. Drain.

Pour the base ingredients over the celery, carrots, corn, and potatoes in a medium pot on low heat. Add the remaining salt (approximately 1/2 tsp) and 1 tbsp bacon grease to saute the onions and garlic. Continue to stir the ingredients frequently to avoid sticking.

You can mash the potatoes or keep the texture lumpy as they soften. Taste Your Base, savor the rich flavors. Take a moment to appreciate the depth of taste you've created. Bring to a low boil.

Let your soup sit for about 20-30 minutes. Taste Your Base and add additional ingredients as needed.

If you are using rice, prepare it according to the Properly Clean Your Food Before You Cook Section, or your usual way.

Feel free to adjust the flavors and cook more if needed. This is your creation, so make it exactly how you want it. Gradually add the bacon crumbles to the soup or on top of each bowl.

Family's Favorite Cornbread

In many families worldwide, bread, crackers, or rice always accompanies any meal or is eaten alone. This versatile bread recipe can be enjoyed with various dishes just like others would use sourdough bread, rosemary or saltine crackers, or tortillas. Cornbread is another staple for eating with your ideal meal or as a quick, delicious light snack.

INGREDIENTS:
BASE:

- 1 cup all-purpose flour
- 1 cup cornmeal
- 1/2 cup and 2 tbsp brown sugar (packed)
- 1 tsp Kosher or sea salt
- 3 1/2 tsp baking powder

- Sprinkle (approximately 1/2 tsp each) (optional)
    - o Thyme
    - o Basil
    - o Bruschetta
    - o Italian Seasoning
    - o Rosemary

OTHER INGREDIENTS:

- 1 cup coconut milk*
- 1 cup evaporated milk or heavy whipping cream*
- 1/3 cup and 1/3 tsp olive oil
- 1 egg
- 1 tsp sea moss (optional)

NOTE:
*Low-fat option is to substitute the heavy cream or evaporated milk with more coconut milk to reduce your dairy intake. If you use the substitution, reduce the total water intake by 1 cup.

FAMILY'S FAVORITE CORNBREAD (CONTINUED)

READY TO MIX:

Preheat the oven to 385 degrees. Use 1/3 tsp of oil to prepare your baking pan, spreading and coating the pan evenly with your hand. Combine the base ingredients in the above order in a large bowl, ensuring they're mixed well before adding the other ingredients.

Gradually add the other ingredients, including the remaining oil (approximately 1/3 cup), in the order indicated. Thoroughly mix. Pour the ingredients from the bowl into the baking pan.

After cooking for 25 minutes:
1. Turn off the oven.
2. Leave the bread in the pan and oven for 7-10 minutes to settle and brown.
3. Test your bread using a toothpick.

If the pick doesn't come out clean, cook for 5-7 additional minutes. Test the bread again using the pick. If not thoroughly cooked, repeat the process. Then, it's time to enjoy your freshly baked bread!

Groovy Guac

I have something special for you if you're in the mood for a delightful snack, whether as a solo treat or a companion to another delicious dish. This dish pairs perfectly with my Pico Savy Salsa and some of my favorite chips. I've enjoyed it alongside my favorite Mexican dishes, but it always shines with my salsa and chips. If you're not a fan of chips, you can serve it with crunchy vegetables or as a topping for your favorite tacos.

INGREDIENTS:
BASE:

- 1 tsp jalapeño juice
- 1/2 tsp or Sprinkle lemon pepper
- 1/2 tsp or Sprinkle of Kosher or sea salt
- 1/2 tsp or Sprinkle of pepper
- ½ tsp garlic powder
- ½ tsp onion powder
- Sprinkle or pinch of turmeric

OTHER INGREDIENTS:

- 2 large avocados (mashed)
- 1/4 cup cilantro (finely minced)
- 1/4 cup red or white onion (finely minced)
- 1 clove of garlic (finely minced)
- 1/2 tsp ginger (finely minced) - optional
- 1 small tomato (similar to the size of a Roma tomatoes) (optional)

READY TO MIX:

Start by creating your base in a small bowl, following the listed order. Stir thoroughly. The beauty of this recipe is that you can taste your base, ensuring it's suitable for your palate. You're in control of the flavors.

GROOVY GUAC (CONTINUED)

In a medium bowl, mash the avocados with a fork and add the other ingredients, including tomatoes, if you prefer. Once everything is thoroughly mixed, add the base ingredients. Stir and lend until harmoniously combined.

Now, the hardest part is to let the flavors mingle in the refrigerator for 45-60 minutes, building anticipation for the delicious result. Taste Your Base Again. Does it hit the right notes for your taste buds?

If not, don't hesitate to tweak the ingredients. You can add more salt for a savory kick or a squeeze of lime for a tangy twist. Keep adjusting until it's perfect for you but with each additional let it settle for at least 10-15 minutes.

Jerky Jerk Chicken

Did you know that listening to your body will tell you what you're missing or craving? Really?! Depending on my body's desires, I may eat my jerk chicken alone as a side dish or as a main dish with other foods I enjoy, like my Kale Salad, Mac and Cheese, Broccoli Bake, or any of my soups.

Sometimes, I eat light all day and then require comfort food later. I let my body decide what fuel it needs for the day and when, but I try not to eat past 3 p.m. or 5 p.m. at the latest. This dish is simple and easy to make. Consider making this delicious, juicy dish using wings, thighs, legs, or all of these.

INGREDIENTS:
BASE:

- 1 tsp coriander
- 1 tsp cumin
- 1 tsp ginger
- 1 tsp turmeric
- 1 tsp onion powder
- 1 tsp garlic powder
- 1 tsp rosemary (ground or powder)
- 1 tsp thyme (ground or powder)
- ½ tsp nutmeg (ground)
- ½ tsp allspice (ground)
- ½ tsp cinnamon (ground)
- 2 tbsp brown sugar
- 1-2 tbsp amino acid (according to taste)
- ½ tsp pepper
- 1 tbsp sea or kosher salt
- 1 tbsp oil olive
- 1 tbsp scotch bonnet, hot pepper sauce, pineapple scotch bonnet, or pineapple habanero jam (depending upon your taste)

OTHER INGREDIENTS:

- 2-3 lbs chicken wings, thighs, or legs or a batch of all three
- ½ tbsp olive oil (for baking)

JERKY JERK CHICKEN (CONTINUED)

READY TO MIX:

Mix the base ingredients except ½ tsp olive oil and scotch bonnet in a large bowl and thoroughly stir. Let the base sit for 30 minutes to infuse the flavors. Taste Your Base to determine if the flavor suits your needs.

Gradually add the scotch bonnet according to taste but not exceeding the suggested amount. Let everything sit for 15 minutes. Taste Your Base. If more flavor is needed or you desire more sweet or hot, gradually add ingredients until you reach the desired flavors.

You can clean your meat any way you desire or go to the Properly Clean Your Food Before You Cook page to learn another way. After you have cleaned the meat:

1. Pat it dry and place the pieces into the base ingredients bowl.
2. Massage each piece thoroughly with the base ingredients.
3. Let the meat sit in the base ingredients for about 20 minutes.

Use a cast iron skillet or cast iron flat plate, and use ½ tsp olive oil to coat either skillet or plate. Place meat on the coated surface and slowly cook at 375 degrees for about 35-40 minutes. Or, if it is a great day, place them on the grill.

Cut off the oven and let it sit for 7-10 minutes. Use a thermometer to ensure it is at 165 degrees, and cut a small slit into the meatiest part of the chicken to ensure it is cooked thoroughly but still juicy. Enjoy!

Nibble's Mac -n- Cheese

> Many families love macaroni and Cheese. However, I do not eat this dish much due to its heartiness. I try to balance my diet, but this is one of my go-to dishes when I want comfort food and crank it up.

INGREDIENTS:
BASE:
- 2 cups heavy cream
- 1.5 cups Havarti Cheese (shredded)
- 1.5 cups Asiago Cheese (shredded)
- ½ tsp salt
- 1 tsp ginger (ground)
- 1 tbsp Italian seasoning (ground)
- 1 tbsp basil seasoning (ground)
- ½ tsp red chili pepper (ground)
- ½ tsp paprika
- 1.5 tsp sea moss or 1.5 tsp flour (optional for thickening)
- 1 cup hot water (optional)

OTHER INGREDIENTS:
- 1 (8 oz) package elbow macaroni
- 2.5 cups water
- ½ tsp salt
- 1 tsp olive oil
- ½ cup bread crumbs

NOTE:

The base ingredients will thicken but will be absorbed by the macaroni once poured over it, so use the flour or sea moss sparingly.

READY TO MIX:
Add the base ingredients as listed on low heat, stirring until the Cheese has melted and everything blends beautifully. It's essential to Taste Your Base at this point.

NIBBLE'S MAC N CHEESE (CONTINUED)

READY TO MIX (CONTINUED)

Let it sit for about 15-20 minutes to thicken, taking responsibility for the final flavor and texture.

Take your time to Taste Your Base again. Add more ingredients gradually, adjusting to your taste. If you prefer a thicker base, add the sea moss or flour in small increments, giving you control over the texture.

Stir thoroughly and let everything sit for about 7 minutes. Then, Taste Your Base to determine if something else is needed, including whether it's thick enough. If you require a thinner base, gradually add water.

Bring about 2.5 cups of water with ½ tsp salt and 1 tsp olive oil to a boil. The salt enhances the flavor of the macaroni, and the olive oil prevents the noodles from sticking together. Then add macaroni to the pot of boiling water on medium heat. Continue to stir and bring to another boil. The noodles should be al dente.

Drain the macaroni, then layer it in a casserole dish. Pour the base ingredients over the macaroni, then add 1 tbsp of bread crumbs. Repeat. Add the remaining bread crumbs (approximately 1 tbsp) at the top.

Bake in the oven at 350 degrees for about 20 minutes. After the stated time, cut off the stove and let the dish remain in the oven for 10-15 minutes to brown. This process is straightforward and will give you a perfectly baked macaroni and cheese.

No Chicken Noodle Soup

Chicken Noodle Soup is a healthy choice, reassuring you of its nutritional benefits. You can create this recipe with or without coconut milk. I use milk due to its creamy texture, which I like in my soups sometimes. This recipe is excellent due to its healthy properties, from combating ailments, improving joint health, and enhancing sleep patterns, to reducing inflammation but without the chicken.

INGREDIENTS:

BASE:

- 1/2 cup Chicken and 1/2 cup Vegetable bouillon or 4 (14.5 oz) cans chicken broth and 1 (14.5 oz) can vegetable broth*
- 3-4 cups Hot Water (depending upon taste)*
- 1 cup onion (finely chopped)
- 1 tbsp garlic (minced or finely chopped)
- 1 tbsp Olive Oil
- 1/2 tsp jalapeño juice
- ½ cup coconut milk
- 1 tbsp amino acid
- 1 tsp cumin
- 1 tsp ground ginger
- 1/2 tsp paprika
- 1/2 tsp lemon pepper
- 1 tsp turmeric
- 1 tsp dried or fresh basil
- 1 tsp dried oregano
- 1 tsp dried or fresh thyme
- 2-4 Bay Leaves
- 1 tbsp sea moss (optional)

OTHER INGREDIENTS:

- 1 1/2 cups carrots (sliced or small carrots cut in half))
- 1 cup celery (finely chopped)
- ½ tsp kosher or sea salt
- 4 cups (8 oz) Penne Pasta, Egg Noodles, or Any Pasta inc Gluten Free

NO CHICKEN NOODLE SOUP (CONTINUED)

NOTE:
*Bouillon is preferred for this dish because it allows you to control the taste. Canned broths will not negate the flavors, but you may have to add salt. If you do not use the bouillon but instead broth, reduce the total water intake by 1 cup.

If using bouillon, mix with hot water, ensuring the flavors blend harmoniously. If needed, add more water or bouillon to achieve the perfect balance.

READY TO MIX:
Begin your culinary journey by delicately sautéing garlic and onions in ½ tbsp of olive oil in a small skillet for a few seconds. In a pot, gradually add the base ingredients, building the flavors step by step. This simple yet effective process ensures you create a delicious base for your soup and showcases your cooking skills.

Taste Your Base. Add the sautéed vegetables to the broth or bouillon and water mixture, make sure that you determine the amount of water-based upon whether using broth or bouillon. Stir thoroughly and Taste Your Base. Your taste buds are your best guide in this culinary journey.

Cook pasta as directed on the box or put the remaining olive oil (1/2 tbsp) and ¼ tsp salt in a large pot of water. Bring water to a boil. Add pasta and cook to al dente (between firm and soft) consistency.

Drain the pasta and add it to the base ingredients, carrots, and celery on medium heat. Continue to stir. Taste Your Base.

NO CHICKEN NOODLE SOUP (CONTINUED)

Now, it's time to put your personal touch on the soup. Does it have the exact taste you're aiming for at this stage? If not, add more ingredients until you gradually achieve the perfect balance. Remember, you're in control of the final taste of your soup.

Cook on medium heat for 15-20 minutes, stirring occasionally to prevent the pasta from sticking. Bring everything to a light boil. Taste Your Base. Add extra ingredients if necessary. Enjoy!

Pico Savy Salsa

> Cooking is an excellent way to relax and enjoy yourself. And when you're in the mood for a light snack, this Salsa treat is a perfect choice. So, why not have fun in the kitchen and whip up this delicious snack with your favorite tortilla chips or my guacamole?

INGREDIENTS:
BASE:

- ½ tbsp lime juice or 1/2 tbsp small fresh lime (squeezed)
- ½ tsp turmeric
- ½ tsp ginger powder
- ½ tsp garlic powder
- ½ tsp onion powder
- 1/2 tsp lemon pepper
- 1/2 tsp Kosher or sea salt
- 1/2 tsp black pepper

OTHER INGREDIENTS:

- 5-7 tomatoes (equates to about 2 cups) finely diced
- 1/4 cup cilantro (minced)
- 1/4 cup red, white, green onion or shallots (minced)
- 1 clove garlic (finely minced)
- 1 jalapeño pepper (minced) or ¼ cup juice

READY TO MIX:

Mix your base ingredients in a small bowl in the order listed. Taste Your Base. Next, add the tomatoes, cilantro, onion, garlic, and jalapeno to a medium bowl. Mix thoroughly.

Slowly pour the base ingredients from the small bowl over the ingredients in the medium bowl. Stir and blend thoroughly. Let the ingredients settle in the refrigerator for 45-60 minutes.

Remember, this recipe is just a starting point. Taste Your Base. Does it have the flavors you desire? If not, feel free to add whatever taste you want. This recipe is all about your personal preferences.

Turkey Kale Potato Soup

If you're a fan of Olive Garden's Pork Zappa Soup, you're in for a treat. I'm not a big meat eater, especially pork, but I love a flavorful soup packed with spices and texture. I've created this dish using ground turkey, but you can also use ground lamb. The process of making this dish was a joy for me, and I'm sure you'll find it enjoyable, too. So, relax and enjoy the journey!

INGREDIENTS:
BASE:

- 4 (8 oz) cans or 3 (12) oz cans) Chicken Broth or ½ cup Chicken bouillon*
- ½ cup Beef Broth or 1-2 tsps Beef bouillon*
- 5 cups of water or more (depending upon taste) *
- 2 cups coconut milk**
- 2 cups heavy cream or evaporated milk**
- 1 tsp garlic powder
- 1 tsp onion powder
- 1/4 tsp turmeric
- Sprinkled flakes of cayenne pepper, crushed pepper, or paprika***

OTHER INGREDIENTS:

- 1 package (around 16 oz) ground turkey or your favorite ground meat
- 2 cups kale (finely chopped)
- 3 large (white or purple sweet) potato or yam (chopped)

TURKEY INGREDIENTS:

- 1 tsp oregano (dried)
- 1 tsp cilantro (finely chopped)
- 1/4 red and 1/4 white onion (finely chopped)
- 1 garlic clove (minced)
- 1/4 tsp cumin
- 1/4 tsp coriander
- 1 tsp ginger (minced or powder)
- 1 tsp garlic powder
- 1 tsp onion powder
- 1/2 tsp Italian seasoning
- 1/2 tsp thyme (ground)
- 1 tsp bruschetta
- 1 tsp rosemary (ground)
- 1 tsp sea or kosher salt
- 3 tbsp olive oil
- 1/4 cup bread crumbs
- 1 tsp lavender (fresh finely chopped) optional

TURKEY KALE POTATO SOUP (CONTINUED)

NOTE:
*Bouillon is preferred for this dish because it allows you to control the taste. Canned broths will not negate the flavors, but you may have to add salt. If you do not use the bouillon, reduce the total water intake by 1 cup.

**A low-fat option is to substitute heavy cream or evaporated milk with more coconut milk to reduce your dairy intake. If you use this substitution, reduce the total water intake by 1 cup.

***The crushed or cayenne peppers boost the other flavors; be mindful of how much pepper you use. If you don't like spicy food, use paprika instead. Either way, you will still be able to experience a flavorful dish.

Purple sweet potato or yam will give your dish a slightly sweet taste but not overpowering. It provides many more healthy benefits than a white potato, from blood sugar control to improved digestion, boosting dietary fiber, and reducing inflammation but an acquired taste.

READY TO MIX:
Add ground turkey or your choice of meat, only 1 tbsp of olive oil, lavender if using, and all the turkey ingredients, except for bread crumbs, in the order listed in a medium bowl. Hand mix thoroughly. Cover the bowl and let it sit in the refrigerator overnight or for about four hours.

This is the moment when the magic begins, as you anticipate the flavors slowly and tantalizingly infusing into the meat. The joy of cooking is in this anticipation. After the wait, remove the bowl from the refrigerator and let it sit for about 30 minutes. Then, add the bread crumbs.

TURKEY KALE POTATO SOUP (CONTINUED)

Next, put the potatoes in the oven at 395 degrees for 30-40 minutes or until soft but not mushy. Test the potatoes' softness using a toothpick. If the toothpick quickly goes through the potatoes easily, they're ready. If not, allow them to cook a few more minutes. Peel the skin off the potatoes and chop them up.

Add the two remaining tablespoons of olive oil to a skillet and brown the meat, chopping it with a fork or wooden spatula to keep it chunky. Cook on low to medium heat until no pink is present but still juicy (estimated 5-7 minutes). Add all of the base ingredients in the order listed in a pot, along with three cups of water using bouillon and no water using broth unless needed. Stir thoroughly on low heat. Bring to a boil. Taste Your Base.

Now, we come to a crucial step. It's essential to get the foundation of your soup just right, and this step sets the stage for the rest of the cooking process. Remember that you still need to add the meat, kale, and potatoes, all of which will bring their flavors.

So, wait before you adjust the broth, bouillon, or pepper flavors. Add the kale to the base, thoroughly stir, and bring to a light boil. Let everything sit for about 10 minutes, then Taste Your Base.

Next, add the chopped potatoes to the base. Now, add the meat to the base ingredients. Mix thoroughly and bring to a light boil. Taste Your Base. Is it too salty and requires additional water? If it' not seasoned enough, gradually add broth, bouillon, and/or water.

TURKEY KALE POTATO SOUP (CONTINUED)

If you want it spicier, add progressively crushed or cayenne pepper. Let the base settle for about 20 minutes, then taste again. How does it taste?

Mix thoroughly and bring to another boil. As the dish boils, it will begin to thicken, and all the flavors will fuse and blend, creating a beautiful medley. Usually, nothing is needed at this point.

Taste Your Base, and if you need anything else, do so gradually. Enjoy!

Jamaican & Nigerian Oxtail Stew

Occasionally, I love to eat foods from Africa and the Caribbean Islands. I thoroughly enjoy the heat and beautiful spices; the smell is irresistible. I learned to cook this dish to satisfy my need to feel like I am on vacation. The beauty of this dish is its versatility you can create it without meat, using spinach, okra, or everything based on your desired taste for the stew that day. It's a canvas for your culinary creativity.

This stew tastes like Africa or the Caribbean Islands, where everything is fresh and nothing is compromised. The quality of the ingredients makes a significant difference. I can tell the difference between eating this dish abroad and in the States. In the States, I visit ethnic markets specializing in the necessary ingredients for these dishes, and I am never disappointed. The freshness of the ingredients is key to the authentic flavors.

INGREDIENTS:
BASE:
- 2 large red onion (minced)
- 2 cloves garlic (minced)
- 4-6 sweet peppers or 2 red bell peppers (minced)
- 1 (20 oz can) tomato paste
- 2 tbsp garlic powder
- 1 tbsp onion powder
- 1 tsp turmeric
- 1 tsp cumin
- 1 tbsp browning sauce
- 1 tsp ginger powder
- 1 tbsp curry powder or yellow curry paste
- 1 tsp beef **and** 1 tsp chicken bouillon
- 3 cups of hot water
- 2 sprigs of thyme or 1 tbsp powder of thyme
- 1/3 cup & 1 tsp olive or grapeseed oil
- ½ cup scotch bonnet hot sauce or 2-3 scotch bonnet peppers (depending upon how much heat you desire)

OTHER INGREDIENTS:
- 2 chicken legs and 2 chicken thighs or about 3-4 cow's legs (optional)
- 1 tbsp kosher or sea salt
- ½ tsp pepper
- 1 tbsp olive oil
- 2 bunches of spinach or 20 pieces of okra OR 1 bunch of spinach and 10 pieces of okra, if you desire, use both - optional

JAMAICAN & NIGERIAN OXTAIL STEW (CONTINUED)

NOTE:
The number of pieces of cow's leg or chicken needed depends on how much meat you desire for your dish. I occasionally cook this dish with meat but sometimes separate the meat pieces from the spinach and/or okra to eat with fufu. Now, let's talk about fufu.

Fufu is a dumpling that is a staple of many African cultures. Hispanic and Latin cultures use tortillas, Asian cultures use rice, and Americans use bread. Using fufu is your choice, but it adds a realistic flavor to the dish. However, if you prefer, you can substitute fufu with rice or enjoy the stew on its own.

The choice is yours, so feel free to eat the dish according to your preferences.

READY TO MIX:
You can create this dish with or without meat.

VEGETABLES ONLY:
In a skillet, lightly sauté the onion, garlic, and peppers in 1 tsp olive or grapeseed oil on low heat until slightly soft. Blend the base ingredients, except for the scotch bonnet, in a pot, and add one and a half cups of hot water and the sauteed vegetables. Stir thoroughly to avoid burning.

Cut off the stove. Allow the ingredients to infuse the flavors and thicken the sauce for 20 minutes. Taste Your Base. Gradually add scotch bonnet according to taste. The scotch bonnet adds a unique heat and flavor to the dish, so it's essential to add it gradually and taste as you go. Start with a small amount and adjust according to your spice tolerance.

JAMAICAN & NIGERIAN OXTAIL STEW (CONTINUED)

Let the ingredients sit for another 20 minutes. Now, it's time to Taste Your Base. Take a small spoonful of the stew and assess the balance of flavors.

This step is crucial as it allows you to determine if the flavor suits your needs and ensure it is not too salty or hot. If more flavor or water is needed, gradually add until you reach the desired flavors. Your taste buds are the final judge, so trust them and adjust as needed.

Next, add spinach, okra, or both to your pot. Continue to cook and thoroughly stir to avoid sticking. Bring to a low boil. Let everything sit for about 20 minutes. Taste Your Base. If you need to add anything, do so gradually according to taste.

OR

WITH MEAT:
If you are using meat, clean it as stated on the Properly Clean Your Food Before You Cook page or as you would usually clean your meat. Season the meat with salt and pepper. Next, add 1 tbsp oil to a skillet on medium heat, add the meat, and slowly brown the meat on all sides.

The following steps are a repeat as stated in preparing the vegetables:
- In a skillet, lightly sauté the onion, garlic, and peppers in 1 tsp olive or grapeseed oil on low heat until slightly soft. Blend the base ingredients, except for the scotch bonnet, in a pot, and add one and a half cups of hot water and the sauteed vegetables. Stir thoroughly.
- Cut off the stove. Allow the ingredients to infuse the flavors and thicken the sauce for 20 minutes. Taste Your Base.

JAMAICAN & NIGERIAN OXTAIL STEW (CONTINUED)

- Gradually add scotch bonnet according to taste. The scotch bonnet adds heat and flavor to your dish, so add gradually and taste as you go.
- Let the ingredients sit for another 20 minutes. Taste Your Base.
- Now, you can determine if the flavor suits your needs and ensure it is not too salty or hot. If more flavor or water is needed, gradually add it until you reach the desired flavor. Your taste buds are the final judge, so trust them and adjust as needed.
- Add spinach, okra, or both to your pot. Continue to cook and thoroughly stir to avoid sticking. Bring to a low boil.
- Let everything sit for about 20 minutes. Taste Your Base. If you need to add anything, do so gradually according to taste.

Add the sauteed meat to the pot, continue to stir, and blend thoroughly to avoid the ingredients from sticking. Bring to a low boil. Let everything sit for about 30 minutes.

Taste Your Base. If needed, add a cup of hot water or any other ingredients. Enjoy!

Japchae

> I saw this dish while watching a gardening and sustainable living documentary. The beautiful colors in this dish were so intriguing that I thought, why not try to see if I can recreate it? I enjoyed getting creative in making this dish work for my needs. If you prefer, you can prepare this dish without meat, which will still be delicious.

INGREDIENTS:

MEAT BASE:

- 2 tbsp amino acid
- ½ tsp rice vinegar
- ½ tsp brown sugar
- 2 tsp sesame oil
- 2 tsp honey
- 2 cloves garlic (minced)
- 1 tsp fresh ginger (minced)
- Pinched of black pepper

NOODLE BASE:

- 1 1/2 tbsp sesame oil
- 2 tsp honey
- 1 tbsp amino acid
- Pinch of salt

VEGETABLE BASE:

- ½ cup amino acid
- ¼ cup plus 1 tsp sesame oil
- 1 tbsp red chili flakes
- 1 tbsp chili paste

EGG BASE:

- 2 medium or large eggs
- ¼ tsp grapeseed or olive oil
- Pinch of salt

OTHER INGREDIENTS:

- 8-10 oz beef (thinly sliced)
- 10 portobello or shitake mushrooms (thinly sliced)
- 1 bunch spinach
- 1 red onion (minced)
- 1 large carrot (minced)
- 1 (6.75-8.8 oz pkg) rice stick noodles
- 2 eggs
- 2 tsp sesame oil
- 1 tbsp sriracha sauce
- 1 clove garlic (minced)
- Pinch of black pepper

JAPCHAE (CONTINUED)

NOTE:
You can always create and refrigerate 2-3x more base ingredients needed later, cutting down your future preparation time. Sometimes, I freeze my sauces if I know I will cook the dish again within the next month or two.

READY TO MIX:
MEAT:
Mix all meat-based ingredients thoroughly in a medium bowl. Let it sit for 20 minutes. Taste Your Base. Add more ingredients if you desire.

Coat the meat-based ingredients and set aside for about 20-30 minutes. Alternatively, you can lightly use my Meat Rub to create more flavorful meat. Remember, use it lightly so it does not overpower the meat-based ingredients you created.

Heat 1 tsp sesame oil on low in a medium skillet, sauté the coated meat, turning it over, for about 5 minutes until tender. Set aside.

VEGETABLES:
Thoroughly mix the base ingredients, and let them sit in a small bowl for 15-20 minutes. Taste Your Base. If it doesn't have the desired taste, add more ingredients.

Set it aside. Add 1 tsp sesame oil to a medium skillet on low heat and add mushrooms, spinach, onions, and carrots. Then, add the vegetables and base ingredients and thoroughly mix in a pot on low heat.

JAPCHAE (CONTINUED)

Continue to stir for about 10 minutes. Taste Your Base to determine if you are reaching the desired taste. If you need to add anything, do so gradually. Cut off the pot and let everything settle for at least 7 minutes.

NOODLES:
In a pot, bring water, a pinch of salt, and ½ tsp sesame oil to a boil. Gradually add noodles and cook until soft, about 4-5 minutes. Drain.

In a small bowl, add the remaining sesame oil (about 1 tsp), honey, and amino acids to the noodles. Taste Your Base. Add more ingredients if needed.

Next, add the cooked noodles to the pot with the meat, vegetables, and base ingredients. Stir thoroughly without any heat. Taste Your Base to determine if anything else is needed.

EGG:
Mix thoroughly eggs and salt in a small bowl. Add ¼ tsp oil to the skillet and the egg mixture on low heat. Scramble lightly.

Add your eggs to the pot—remember, the stove should still be off—along with the meat, vegetables, and base ingredients. Stir thoroughly. Taste Your Base to see if anything else is needed. If anything else is required, including additional sauce, add it gradually.

Lamb In Yogurt Sauce

We don't eat meat often but prefer lamb over beef and chicken. Lamb is lean, tender, easy to digest, and flavorful. As a kid, my eczema prevented me from drinking cow's milk, so goat's milk was ideal, and lamb also became my go-to. Fast-forward, I still love and use goat products. I drink goat's milk, use goat's butter, and occasionally use goat body butter, which keeps the skin soft, supple, and smooth.

INGREDIENTS:
BASE:
- 1 cup coconut milk
- ½ cup garlic (minced) or 1.5 tbsp powder
- ½ cup onion (minced) or 1.5 tbsp onion powder
- 1 tsp turmeric
- ½ tsp black pepper
- 1 tbsp kosher salt
- 1 tsp ginger (minced)
- 1/3 cup Olive oil

SUGGESTED HERBS:
- thyme
- basil
- cilantro
- rosemary
- lavender
- 3-4 sprigs of each fresh herb chosen. Either remove leaves from sprigs or use whole sprigs for up o 5 lbs of leg of lamb or rack of lamb.

OTHER INGREDIENTS:
- 3-5 lbs leg of lamb (bone-in or out, your preference) or rack of lamb
- ¼ cups of red or white wine

KITCHEN SINK:

What type of dairy do you have in your fridge? When preparing this dish, the goal is to add more fat to the meat. The dairy base helps to tenderize and infuse the flavors into the meat.

LAMB IN YOGURT SAUCE (CONTINUED)

If you have sour cream, you can use it instead of coconut milk or ½ cups of coconut milk for ½ cups of sour cream. The choice is yours, but ensure your dairy product totals no more than 1 cup.

NOTE:
If you are considering using this yogurt sauce again with a different type of meat within 90-120 days, prepare more than needed by doubling the ingredients and freezing the excess. You can also use this yogurt sauce as instructed, but cook only half of the meat and freeze the rest.

You can also use Nita's Nibble Rub to season the meat if you desire, but you will still need olive oil and coconut milk available and apply according to the recipe.

Refrigerate the meat for 6-8 hours.*

READY TO MIX:
Add the base ingredients in the above order or the Nita's Nibble Rub in a medium bowl. Let the mix sit for about 45-60 minutes to allow the flavors to meld. Taste Your Base to determine if the flavor suits your needs. If more flavor is needed, gradually add ingredients until you reach the desired flavors.

Next, add the chosen fresh herbs to the base mix and blend thoroughly. Allow the base mix and herbs to sit for 45 minutes and then taste. Does it satisfy your taste buds, or do you believe that you need to add something else? If you are adding gradually, do so.

LAMB IN YOGURT SAUCE (CONTINUED)

Gradually scoop some base mix with your fingers and rub it into the meat, covering all sides. Slit or puncture holes into the meat using a knife or fork and wait 15 minutes for the base to saturate the meat. Gather more base mix with your fingers and add more onto the meat, covering all sides.

Concentrate on getting some base mix and herbs into the puncture holes as you saturate the meat with your fingers. This process helps the flavors penetrate the meat, enhancing its taste. Let the base, herbs, and meat marinate for about 20 minutes.

This allows the flavors to develop further. Wrap the meat in plastic wrap and refrigerate for 6-8 hours* to allow the meat to absorb the flavors thoroughly. Preheat the oven to 385 degrees.

Place the meat in a cooking pan in the oven with about ¼ cups of red or white wine. Cook on one side for about 20 minutes, then turn the meat over to cook for another 20 minutes. Remove the meat from the oven and place it, including the juices, on medium heat in a cast iron skillet on the stove.

In the skillet, put a fork in the meat and circle it around the juices for about 5-7 minutes. Turn the meat over and repeat for another 5-7 minutes. These steps help sear the meat while creating a sauce or gravy that brings all the parts of the dish together. Your meat will still be juicy and a little pink.

Chicken Tikka Masala

This dish, a favorite of mine, is a versatile and nutritious meal that provides the essential protein, curry, and vegetables. I've always been drawn to curry dishes healing properties and delightful flavors. You can pair this dish with parboiled, jasmine, basmati, or brown rice and enjoy it with or without chicken, allowing you to customize it to your liking.

Regardless of your choice, you're in for a delightful cooking experience. If you're craving more sauce, prepare 2-3 times the indicated amount and freeze the extra for future use. The joy of cooking this dish is in your hands.

INGREDIENTS
BASE:

- 3 tsp tikka masala
- 1 ½ tsp garlic powder
- 1 ½ tsp onion powder
- 1 tbsp ginger powder
- 1 tsp cumin
- 1 tsp turmeric
- 2 ½ tsp Kosher salt
- 2 tbsp brown sugar
- 1 (14 oz) can tomato sauce
- 1 tsp paprika or chili powder
- 1 cup chopped red or white onion
- 2 cloves garlic (minced)
- 1 ½ cup coconut milk*
- 1 ½ cups heavy cream or evaporated milk*

MEAT BASE:

- 1 tsp Kosher salt
- 1 tsp garlic powder
- 1 tsp onion powder
- 1 tsp turmeric
- 1 tsp cumin
- 1 tsp coriander
- 1 tsp ginger (minced)
- Pinched of black pepper

OTHER INGREDIENTS

- 4 tsp vegetable or olive oil
- 1 cup water
- 1 clove garlic (minced)
- 1 cup onion (minced)
- 5 lbs or up to five (5) pieces of chicken breast (thinly sliced or bite-sized pieces)
- 1 cup carrots (shredded)
- ½ large red or yellow bell pepper (minced)

CHICKEN TIKKA MASALA (CONTINUED)

NOTE:
*Low-fat option is to substitute the heavy cream or evaporated milk with more coconut milk to reduce your dairy intake. If you use the substitution, reduce the total water intake by 1 cup.

READY TO MIX:
Clean the chicken according to the Properly Clean Your Food Before You Cook page or your preferred method. Pat the chicken dry. Next, thoroughly rub 1 tsp of the oil on the chicken before adding and mixing with the meat-based ingredients.

Cut the meat up as desired, thinly sliced or in bite-sized pieces. Mix all meat-based ingredients thoroughly in a small bowl. Taste Your Base to ensure the flavors are balanced and adjust as needed.

Add more ingredients if you desire. Set the meat-based ingredients aside for about 35 minutes. In a large bowl, coat and thoroughly mix the meat-based ingredients with the cleaned chicken and let it sit for 45 minutes.

Alternatively, you can marinate the meat overnight. Make sure that all of the meat is thoroughly coated. The goal is to infuse all of the flavors together with the meat.

Heat 1 tsp oil in a medium skillet and add meat. Saute the meat continually for a few minutes until all pink is gone outside, but the inside is still juicy and has not dried out. Set aside.

CHICKEN TIKKA MASALA (CONTINUED)

In a medium skillet with 1 tsp oil on low heat, saute the onion and garlic until slightly soft. In a medium bowl, thoroughly mix the base ingredients except water. Add base ingredients to the sauteed onion and garlic in the skillet.

Stir thoroughly for a few minutes. Taste Your Base. Add more ingredients if you desire.

Set the base ingredients aside for about 20-30 minutes. Next, add carrots and peppers to the base ingredients in the skillet. Blend thoroughly. Taste Your Base.

Let everything settle for about 20 minutes. Taste Your Base again to see if anything else needs to be added before adding meat. Add cooked meat and juices to the base ingredients, and gradually add water as needed.

Cook on medium heat for about 15 minutes, stirring occasionally, and bring to a light boil. This step helps cook the meat thoroughly and bring out the flavors. Taste Your Base. Nothing should be added, but do so gradually if needed.

Vegetable Kadai

If you're in the mood for a beautiful and delicious dish with a hint of heat, this one's perfect. It's incredibly comforting during the winter, fall, or cold, chilly days. The best part? You can adjust the heat level to your liking without compromising the flavor. This dish is not just a recipe; it's a canvas for your culinary creativity. I discovered that 'kadai' (or 'kadhai') in Hindi and Urdu means Wok, a vital tool in this recipe.

When I first tasted this dish in an Indian restaurant, I was immediately intrigued. The fact that it was a vegetarian Indian restaurant made it even more enjoyable. I decided to order it, and the experience was unforgettable. The garlic Naan and mango lassi accompanying the meal added to the delight. This sparked my curiosity, and I was determined to recreate this dish according to my liking. I'm sharing this personal journey with you, hoping it will inspire your culinary adventures.

INGREDIENTS:
BASE:
- 1 cup tomato sauce or 1 (8 oz) can tomato paste
- 1 ½ cups water (if using sauce) or 2 cups water (if using paste)
- ½ tbsp brown sugar
- 1 ½ tbsp kosher salt
- 1 tsp tikki masala powder
- 1/2 tsp turmeric powder
- 2 cups heavy whipping cream
- 1 tsp coriander powder (or seeds)
- 2 tsp cumin powder (or seeds)
- 1 tsp chili powder or flakes
- 1/2 tsp black pepper
- 1/2 tsp fennel seeds
- 1-2 tbsp sea moss (optional)

VEGETABLES:
- 1/2 cup red onion (chopped)
- 1/2 cup white onion (chopped)
- 2-3 shallots (chopped)
- 1 tbsp garlic (grated or minced)
- 1 tsp ginger (grated or minced
- 1 carrot (chopped chunky)
- 1 medium (white or purple sweet) potato or yam (chopped)
- 1/2 cup green beans (or snap peas)
- 1 small head of cauliflower (chopped chunky)
- 1 small head of broccoli (chopped chunky)
- 1/2 cup of red bell pepper (chopped chunky)
- 1/2 cup olive oil (inc 1 tbsp for vegetable sautee)

VEGETABLE KADAI (CONTINUED)

KITCHEN SINK:
Feel free to experiment with the vegetables you add. You can add almost any vegetable around the house, but just be mindful of what you add. You want to maintain the dish's integrity without compromising or overpowering it.

For example, the flavors of celery or squash may be too overpowering for this dish. Don't be afraid to try new combinations and see what works best for you.

NOTE:
Instead of seeds, use the powder, but if desired, you can temper the seeds (cumin, coriander, and fennel) to enhance their flavors before mixing with the other base ingredients. I've tried to temper many of the seeds in the past but have yet to be successful. I met a wonderful Eastern Indian lady in an ethnic market who told me how to do it properly and the benefits of tempering the seeds, but I have had no success yet.

The veggies should be chunky in this dish, but you can slice or prepare them according to your preference.

Purple sweet potato or yam will give your dish a slightly sweet taste but not overpowering. It provides many more healthy benefits than a white potato, from blood sugar control to improved digestion, boosting dietary fiber, and reducing inflammation but is an acquired taste.

VEGETABLE KADAI (CONTINUED)

READY TO MIX:

Mix the base ingredients thoroughly in a medium bowl and let it sit for about 10 minutes. Taste Your Base. Add everything to the Wok on low heat. Continually stir to avoid sticking until it comes to a light boil. Gradually add ½ cups of water.

Taste Your Base to determine if you need to add water. Does it have the flavors you desire? You should be able to taste all the beautiful flavors with a hint of a spicy kick. If not, gradually adjust the ingredients, including water, to suit your taste.

Remove the base ingredients from the Wok and add 1 tbsp of olive oil. Gradually add all of your vegetables and lightly saute. Blend thoroughly. Pour the base ingredients over the vegetables and thoroughly mix until they come to a light boil.

Let everything sit for 15-20 minutes. Taste Your Base to see if you have acquired the desired taste. If so, add gradually, including water, if needed.

Vegetable Thai Yellow Curry

I love spicy foods, and as a foodie, I enjoy all types of foods. This yellow Thai Curry dish is perfect for those who prefer a milder spice level. The red curry is ordinarily hot, similar to hot sauce, while the green is spicy. As you might have noticed, I often incorporate a variety of chilies and curries into my dishes.

Yellow curry is a prime example of its unique turmeric, lemongrass, and cumin blend. What's truly fascinating about this dish is its versatility, bridging the gap between different culinary cultures. For example, earlier this month, I prepared Vegetable Kadhi, which had a slightly different flavor because it was Indian-inspired, but many of the ingredients were similar to this dish. This dish is delicious whether you like Thai or Indian food. Enjoy!

INGREDIENTS:
BASE:
- 4-5 garlic cloves (minced)
- 5 shallots (minced)
- 1/2 cup cilantro (minced)
- 1 tbsp coriander powder
- 1 tsp cumin powder*
- 1 tsp raw turmeric (minced or powder)*
- 1/2 tsp raw ginger (minced)
- 2 stalks lemongrass (minced)*
- 1 tbsp chili pepper
- 1 tbsp lime juice

OTHER INGREDIENTS:
- 2-4 cups coconut milk**
- 2-4 cups heavy whipping cream**
- 2 cups of hot water or 3 cups (curry paste)
- 1 tbsp sesame oil
- 1 tbsp peanut sauce
- 1 tsp brown sugar
- 1 tsp sea salt
- 1 tbsp sea moss (optional)
- 1 tbsp fresh basil (chopped)
- 1/2 cup of each (chopped):
    Onion
    Carrots
    Cauliflower
    Broccoli
    Snap peas
    Potato (red or purple sweet or yam)
    Bell Pepper

VEGETABLE THAI YELLOW CURRY (CONTINUED)

KITCHEN SINK:
Feel free to experiment with the vegetables you add. You can add almost any vegetable around the house, but just be mindful of what you add. You want to maintain the dish's integrity without compromising or overpowering it.

For example, the flavors of celery or squash may be too overpowering for this dish. Feel free to try new combinations and see what works best for you.

NOTE:
*This dish allows you to create your yellow curry paste using turmeric, lemongrass, and cumin. If you're pressed for time, you can buy it from brands like Mae Ploy, Thai Kitchen, or any other type. However, read the ingredients to ensure they have these ingredients to avoid duplication if you buy curry paste.

Due to the thickness of the paste, you may need to add water in most cases. If so, do it gradually. Taste Your Base to create the right balance.

**Low-fat option is to substitute the heavy cream or evaporated milk with more coconut milk to reduce your dairy intake.

Purple sweet potato or yam will give your dish a slightly sweet taste but not overpowering. It provides many more healthy benefits than a white potato, from blood sugar control to improved digestion, boosting dietary fiber, and reducing inflammation but an acquired taste.

If you want more sauce, prepare 2-3 times more of the indicated ingredients for later use. This sauce is ideal over rice, mashed, or baked potatoes.

VEGETABLE THAI YELLOW CURRY (CONTINUED)

READY TO MIX:
OPTION 1:
To create your yellow curry paste:
1. Combine and stir all base ingredients, except water, in a medium pot on low heat.
2. Place the ingredients in a blender, gradually adding 1/2 cup coconut milk, 1/2 cup heavy whipping cream, and, if using, 1/2 tbsp sea moss. If you are making any dairy substitutions do so here.

Also, adjust your dish using an equal amount of coconut milk and heavy cream (Example: 1/4 cup of coconut milk and 1/4 cup of heavy cream) to minimize the sugar, salt, or spice. But if you want it sweetened, gradually add brown sugar, stir thoroughly, let the sugar dissolve, and set for about seven minutes. Taste Your Base.

3. Bring to a low boil.
4. Let it sit for 20 minutes, then Taste Your Base.

Are you achieving the flavors you desire? Is it too spicy, salty, or sweet? Gradually add whatever you need to achieve the perfect balance, including water. Remember, balance is key to creating a delicious yellow curry.

If you feel the dish needs more salt, add it gradually. Let it dissolve and set for about seven minutes. Remember, the flavors will continue to develop, so take it slow before adding anything else. Trust your taste buds and adjust the dish to fit your liking.

5. Add water or whatever other ingredients are needed at this point.
6. Gradually add the other ingredients except for the vegetables.

VEGETABLE THAI YELLOW CURRY (CONTINUED)

7. Add the vegetables and blend thoroughly on low heat for about 15 minutes. Let it sit for about 10 minutes. Taste Your Base.
8. Add another 1/2 cup of coconut milk, 1/2 cup heavy whipping cream, and the remainder of the sea moss if you use it.
9. Let it sit for 20 minutes, then Taste Your Base.

OPTION 2:

Take 4 tbsp of store-bought curry paste in a medium skillet on low heat with 2-3 cups each of coconut milk and heavy cream, then add 1/2 tbsp sea moss, if using. If you are using a dairy substitution, do so at this point to stay within the total amount. Taste Your Base.

Let it sit for 20 minutes. Taste Your Base. Gradually add the other ingredients except for the vegetables, then add another 1/2 cup of coconut milk, 1/2 cup heavy whipping cream, and the remainder of the sea moss if using it on low heat. Let it sit for another 20 minutes.

Adjust using an equal amount of coconut milk and heavy cream (Example: 1/4 cup of coconut milk and 1/4 cup of heavy cream) to minimize the sugar, salt, or spice. But if you want it sweeter, add brown sugar, stir thoroughly, let the sugar dissolve, and sit for seven minutes. Taste Your Base.

Are you obtaining the flavors that you want so far? Is it too spicy, salty, or sweet? Gradually add whatever you need for the desired taste, even water.

If more curry paste is necessary, gradually add it, but Taste Your Base along the way. Add the vegetables and blend thoroughly on low heat for about 15 minutes. Let it sit for about 10 minutes. Taste Your Base.

ACKNOWLEDGMENTS

I am deeply grateful to the Most High God for the life experiences that have guided me towards a healthy and sustainable lifestyle.

I am honored that you are interested in hearing my story, and I know it will be a blessing to you and your well-being. This is an ongoing journey, and my primary focus is to contribute to change consciously. Change is not possible without thoughtful consideration, concerted effort, and decisive actions.

It's a common belief that we should wait for others to initiate change, but we must understand that it starts with us. Each of us has the power to make a difference through our personal choices and actions. Every individual plays a crucial role in how we positively engage with the environment. Our combined efforts will benefit Mother Earth and serve as a valuable asset for the present and the future.

John McKinney has always told me that I was a storyteller, and then others began to follow suit and label me the same. I have been telling stories that have interested people for many decades in various forms. When I started creating this book, which had been burning in my heart for years, I wanted to tell the story of my decades of high-energy, healthy eating and sustainable living that others were always curious about, which began during my childhood, thanks to my parents.

My journey would not have been complete without the efforts of several people, especially my daughter, Nikita. I love and thank everyone that has been such a blessing to and for me. This book is a collection of my experiences and a practical guide for anyone who wants to live their best life while being a better version of themselves!

I saved the best for last: my parents. Because of them, this book exists. Despite my opposition to cooking, my mom was the vessel for beginning my cooking journey because she knew I needed these survival skills. I truly appreciate her for this.

My dad was the backbone of our family, including his siblings, nephews, and nieces. Dad, we will all miss you. Rest in Peace.

WHO IS NITA'S NIBBLES

Vernita Whitaker Naylor, mother, daughter, sister, auntie, friend, foodie, storyteller, life enthusiast, world traveler, small business advocate, entrepreneur, motivator, author.......LIVING HER BEST LIFE!

INDEX

A

ALLSPICE
- Bread Pudding, 70-72
- Heavenly Golden Milk, 62
- Homemade Apple Pie, 73-75
- Jerky Jerk Chicken, 117-118
- Meat Rub, 91
- Oatmeal Spice Cookies, 78-80
- Spice Granola Mix, 83-85

ARTICHOKE & SPINACH DIP & SPREAD, 95-96

B

BAKED POTATO SOUP, 97-100

BASIL
- Baked Potato Soup, 97-100
- Brine, 89
- Butternut Squash Soup, 104-108
- Family's Favorite Cornbread, 112-113
- Lamb in Yogurt Sauce, 139-142
- Meat Rub, 91
- Nibble's Mac N Cheese, 119-120
- Nita's Nibbles Rub, 92
- Nita's Nibbles **Spicy!** Rub, 93
- No Chicken Noodle Soup, 121-123
- Vegetable Thai Yellow Curry, 149-153

BEVERAGES
- Healthy Immunity Tonic, 63-64
- Heavenly Golden Milk, 62
- Hibiscus Tonic, 66-67
- Hot Toddy Tonic (For Kids), 65

INDEX

BEVERAGES (CONTINUED)
    Mango Lassi, 68

BOOKS
    Back to Eden by Jethro Kloss, 31
    Eat Right For Your Blood Type by Dr. Peter J. D'Adamo, 31
    Healing Secrets of the Native Americans: Herbs, Remedies, and Practices that Restore the Body, Refresh the Mind, and Rebuild the Spirit by Porter Shimer, 31

BREAD PUDDING, 70-72

BRINE, RUBS & SAUCES
    Brine, 89
    How to Use Brine, Rub & Sauces, 87-88
    Japanese Ginger Sauce, 90
    Meat Rub, 91
    Nita's Nibbles Rub, 92
    Nita's Nibbles Spicy! Rub, 93

BROCCOLI BAKE, 101-103

BUTTERNUT SQUASH SOUP, 104-108

C

CAYENNE & CHILI PEPPER
    Baked Potato Soup, 97-100
    Butternut Squash Soup, 104-108
    Corn Chowder, 109-111
    Healthy Immunity Tonic, 63-64
    Hot Toddy Tonic (For Kids), 65
    Japchae, 136-138
    Nibble's Mac N Cheese, 119-120
    Nita's Nibbles Spicy! Rub, 93

INDEX

CAYENNE & CHILI PEPPER (CONTINUED)
    Turkey Kale Potato Soup, 126-128
    Vegetable Kadai, 146-148
    Vegetable Thai Yellow Curry, 149-153

CHICKEN TIKKA MASALA, 143-145

CINNAMON
    Bread Pudding, 70-72
    Butternut Squash Soup, 104-108
    Heavenly Golden Milk, 62
    Homemade Apple Pie, 73-75
    Jerky Jerk Chicken, 117-118
    Mango Lassi, 68
    Meat Rub, 91
    Nita's Nibbles **Spicy!** Rub, 93
    Oatmeal Spice Cookies, 78-80
    Spice Granola Mix, 83-85

CORN CHOWDER, 109-111

CULTURE
    Chicken Tikka Masala, 143-145
    Jamaican & Nigerian Oxtail Stew, 131-134
    Japchae, 136-138
    Jerky Jerk Chicken, 117-118
    Nibble's Mac N Cheese, 119-120
    Vegetable Kadai, 146-148
    Vegetable Thai Yellow Curry, 149-153

CUMIN
    Chicken Tikka Masala, 143-145
    Jamaican & Nigerian Oxtail Stew, 131-134

INDEX

CUMIN (CONTINUED)
    Jerky Jerk Chicken, 117-118
    Meat Rub, 91
    Nita's Nibbles Rub, 92
    Nita's Nibbles Spicy! Rub, 93
    No Chicken Noodle Soup, 121-123
    Turkey Kale Potato Soup, 126-128
    Vegetable Kadai, 146-148
    Vegetable Thai Yellow Curry, 149-153

CURRY
    Jamaican & Nigerian Oxtail Stew, 131-134
    Meat Rub, 91
    Nita's Nibbles Rub, 92
    Nita's Nibbles Spicy! Rub, 93
    Vegetable Thai Yellow Curry, 149-153

D
DESSERTS, See SWEETS, 69

E
ENTREES, See MAIN DISHES, 130

F
FAMILY'S FAVORITE CORNBREAD, 112-113

G
GARDENING & SUSTAINABILITY, 39-43
GARLIC (inc Powder)
    Artichoke & Spinach Dip & Spread, 95-96
    Baked Potato Soup, 97-100
    Brine, 89
    Broccoli Bake, 101-103

INDEX

GARLIC (inc POWDER) (CONTINUED)
- Butternut Squash, 104-108
- Chicken Tikka Masala, 143-145
- Corn Chowder Soup, 109-111
- Groovy Gauc, 114-116
- Healthy Immunity Tonic, 63-64
- Hot Toddy Tonic (For Kids), 65
- Jamaican & Nigerian Oxtail Stew, 131-134
- Japanese Ginger Sauce, 90
- Japchae, 136-138
- Jerky Jerk Chicken, 117-118
- Lamb in Yogurt Sauce, 139-142
- Meat Rub, 91
- Nita's Nibbles Rub, 92
- Nita's Nibbles Spicy! Rub, 93
- No Chicken Noodle Soup, 121-123
- Pico Savy Salsa, 124
- Turkey Kale Potato Soup, 125-129
- Vegetable Kadai, 146-148
- Vegetable Thai Yellow Curry, 149-153

GINGER
- Baked Potato Soup, 97-100
- Brine, 89
- Butternut Squash, 104-108
- Chicken Tikka Masala, 143-145
- Heavenly Golden Milk, 62
- Groovy Gauc, 114-116
- Healthy Immunity Tonic, 63-64

INDEX

GINGER (CONTINUED)
    Hibiscus Tonic, 66-67
    Hot Toddy Tonic (For Kids), 65
    Jamaican & Nigerian Oxtail Stew, 131-134
    Japanese Ginger Sauce, 90
    Japchae, 136-138
    Jerkey Jerk Chicken, 117-118
    Lamb in Yogurt Sauce, 139-142
    Meat Rub, 91
    Nibble's Mac N Cheese, 119-120
    Nita's Nibbles Rub, 92
    Nita's Nibbles **Spicy!** Rub, 93
    No Chicken Noodle Soup, 121-123
    Pico Savy Salsa, 124
    Turkey Kale Potato Soup, 125-129
    Vegetable Kadai, 146-148
    Vegetable Thai Yellow Curry, 149-153

GOING BACK TO BASICS, 31-33

GROOVY GAUC, 114-116

H

HEALTHY IMMUNITY TONIC, 63-64

HEAVENLY GOLDEN MILK, 62

HELPFUL HINTS
    Kitchen Sink, 55-56
    Note, 57
    What Flavors Suit You? 58-59

HIBISCUS TONIC, 66-67

HOMEMADE APPLE PIE, 73-75

INDEX

HOT TODDY TONIC (FOR KIDS), 65
HOW TO USE BRINE, RUBS & SAUCES, 87-88

I

IS YOUR BODY INFLAMED?, 34-35
IMPORTANCE OF USING HERBS, SPICES &
    SEA MOSS FOR TEXTURE, 45-47

J

JAMAICAN & NIGERIAN OXTAIL STEW, 131-134
JAPANESE GINGER SAUCE, 90
JAPCHAE, 136-138
JERKY JERK CHICKEN, 117-118
JUICES, See BEVERAGES, 61

K

KITCHEN SINK, 15, 55-56

L

LAMB IN YOGURT SAUCE, 139-142
LEMON PEPPER
    Groovy Gauc, 114-116
    Meat Rub, 91
    Nita's Nibbles Rub, 92
    Nita's Nibbles **Spicy!** Rub, 93
    No Chicken Noodle Soup, 121-123
    Pico Savy Salsa, 124

M

MAIN DISHES
    Chicken Tikka Masala, 143-145
    Jamaican & Nigerian Oxtail Stew, 131-134
    Japchae, 136-138
    Lamb in Yogurt Sauce, 139-142

INDEX

MAIN DISHES (CONTINUED)
    Vegetable Kadai, 146-148
    Vegetable Thai Yellow Curry, 149-153

MANGO LASSI, 68

MEAT RUB, 91

MEAT DISHES
    Chicken Tikka Masala, 143-145
    Jamaican & Nigerian Oxtail Stew, 131-134
    Jerky Jerk Chicken, 117-118
    Lamb in Yogurt Sauce, 139-142
    Turkey Kale Potato Soup, 125-129

N

NIBBLE'S MAC N CHEESE, 119-120

NITA'S BUTTERMILK LEMONY LOAF, 76-77

NITA'S NIBBLES RUB, 92

NITA'S NIBBLES SPICY! RUB, 93

NO CHICKEN NOODLE SOUP, 121-123

NON-DAIRY (inc Coconut Milk)
    Baked Potato Soup, 97-100
    Butternut Squash, 104-108
    Chicken Tikka Masala, 143-145
    Corn Chowder Soup, 109-111
    Family's Favorite Cornbread, 112-113
    Heavenly Golden Milk, 62
    Lamb In Yogurt Sauce, 139-142
    Mango Lassi, 68
    No Chicken Noodle Soup, 121-123
    Turkey Kale Potato Soup, 125-129
    Vegetable Thai Yellow Curry, 149-153

INDEX

NUTMEG
- Bread Pudding, 70-72
- Heavenly Golden Milk, 62
- Homemade Apple Pie, 73-75
- Jerky Jerk Chicken, 117-118
- Mango Lassi, 68
- Meat Rub, 91
- Oatmeal Spice Cookies, 78-80
- Spice Granola Mix, 83-85

O

OATMEAL SPICE COOKIES, 78-80

OREGANO
- Baked Potato Soup, 97-100
- Brine, 89
- Butternut Squash, 104-108
- Corn Chowder Soup, 109-111
- Lamb in Yogurt Sauce, 139-142
- Meat Rub, 91
- No Chicken Noodle Soup, 121-123
- Turkey Kale Potato Soup, 125-129

P

PAPRIKA
- Baked Potato Soup, 97-100
- Butternut Squash Soup, 104-108
- Corn Chowder, 109-111
- Meat Rub, 91
- Nibble's Mac N Cheese, 119-120
- No Chicken Noodle Soup, 121-123
- Turkey Kale Potato Soup, 125-129

INDEX

PICO SAVY SALSA, 124

PINEAPPLE UPSIDE-DOWN CAKE, 81-82

PREPARATION & COOK TIME, 51-53

PROPERLY CLEAN YOUR FOOD BEFORE YOU COOK, 48-50

R

ROSEMARY

    Brine, 89

    Butternut Squash, 104-108

    Corn Chowder Soup, 109-111

    Family's Favorite Cornbread, 112-113

    Jerky Jerk Chicken, 117-118

    Lamb in Yogurt Sauce, 139-142

    Meat Rub, 91

    Nita's Nibbles Rub, 92

    Nita's Nibbles Spicy! Rub, 93

    Turkey Kale Potato Delight Soup, 125-129

S

SEA MOSS, 46

    Artichoke & Spinach Dip & Spread, 95-96

    Baked Potato Soup, 97-100

    Broccoli Bake, 101-103

    Butternut Squash, 104-108

    Family's Favorite Cornbread, 112-113

    Healthy Immunity Tonic, 63-64

    Hibiscus Tonic, 66-67

    Hot Toddy Tonic (For Kids), 65

    Nibble's Mac N Cheese, 119-120

    No Chicken Noodle Soup, 121-123

INDEX

SEA MOSS (CONTINUED)
    Vegetable Kadai, 146-148
    Vegetable Thai Yellow Curry, 149-153
SIDES, See STARTERS, 94
SPICE GRANOLA MIX, 83-85
STARTERS
    Artichoke & Spinach Dip & Spread, 95-96
    Baked Potato Soup, 97-100
    Broccoli Bake, 101-103
    Butternut Squash, 104-108
    Corn Chowder Soup, 109-111
    Family's Favorite Cornbread, 112-113
    Groovy Gauc, 114-116
    Jerky Jerk Chicken, 117-118
    Nibble's Mac N Cheese, 119-120
    No Chicken Noodle Soup, 121-123
    Pico Savy Salsa, 124
    Turkey Kale Potato Soup, 125-129
SUSTAINABILITY & GARDENING, 39-43
SWEETS
    Bread Pudding, 70-72
    Homemade Apple Pie, 73-75
    Nita's Buttermilk Lemony Loaf, 76-77
    Oatmeal Spice Cookies, 78-80
    Pineapple Upside Down Cake, 81-82
    Spice Granola Mix, 83-85

T
TASTE YOUR BASE, 14-16, 37

INDEX

THYME
- Brine, 89
- Butternut Squash, 104-108
- Corn Chowder Soup, 109-111
- Family's Favorite Cornbread, 112-113
- Jerky Jerk Chicken, 117-118
- Lamb in Yogurt Sauce, 139-142
- Meat Rub, 91
- No Chicken Noodle Soup, 121-123
- Turkey Kale Potato Delight Soup, 125-129

TURKEY KALE POTATO DELIGHT SOUP, 125-129

TURMERIC
- Baked Potato Soup, 97-100
- Brine, 89
- Butternut Squash, 104-108
- Chicken Tikka Masala, 143-145
- Corn Chowder Soup, 109-111
- Healthy Immunity Tonic, 63-64
- Heavenly Golden Milk, 62
- Groovy Gauc, 114-116
- Hibiscus Tonic, 66-67
- Hot Toddy Tonic (For Kids), 65
- Jamaican & Nigerian Oxtail Stew, 131-134
- Jerky Jerk Chicken, 117-118
- Lamb in Yogurt Sauce, 139-142
- Meat Rub, 91
- Nita's Nibble Rub, 92
- Nita's Nibble **Spicy!** Rub, 93

INDEX

TURMERIC (CONTINUED)
      No Chicken Noodle Soup, 121-123
      Pico Savy Salsa, 124
      Turkey Kale Potato Soup, 125-129
      Vegetable Kadai, 146-148
      Vegetable Thai Yellow Curry, 149-153

V
VEGETABLE KADAI, 146-148
VEGETABLE THAI YELLOW CURRY, 149-153
VEGETABLES
      Artichoke & Spinach Dip & Spread, 95-96
      Baked Potato Soup, 97-100
      Broccoli Bake, 101-103
      Butternut Squash, 104-108
      Corn Chowder Soup, 109-111
      Chicken Tikka Masala, 143-145
      Groovy Gauc, 114-116
      Jamaican & Nigerian Oxtail Stew, 131-134
      Japchae, 136-138
      No Chicken Noodle Soup, 121-123
      Pico Savy Salsa, 124
      Turkey Kale Potato Soup, 125-129
      Vegetable Kadai, 146-148
      Vegetable Thai Yellow Curry, 149-153

W
WHAT FLAVORS SUIT YOU, 58-59

www.ingramcontent.com/pod-product-compliance
Lightning Source LLC
Chambersburg PA
CBHW061158010526
44119CB00059B/855